100 GREATS YORKSHIRE County Cricket Club

Yorkshire's first 'official' Championship-winning team of 1893. From left to right, back row: E. Wainwright, J. Tunnicliffe, H. Turner (scorer), D. Hunter, R. Moorhouse. Middle row: G. Ulyett, F.S. Jackson, Lord Hawke (captain), A. Sellers, R. Peel. Front row: J.T. Brown, E. Smith, G.H. Hirst.

100 GREATS

YORKSHIRE COUNTY CRICKET CLUB

MICK POPE & PAUL DYSON

First published 2001

Tempus Publishing Limited
The Mill, Brimscombe Port,
Stroud, Gloucestershire, GL5 2QG

ISBN 0 7524 2179 4

Typesetting and origination by
Tempus Publishing Limited
Printed in Great Britain by
Midway Colour Print, Wiltshire

Arnie Sidebottom and Jim Love celebrate Yorkshire's thrilling Benson & Hedges Cup final victory over Northamptonshire at Lord's on 11 July 1987.

Key:
The letters at the top of the page refer to the following batting or bowling styles:

RHB – right-handed batsman
LHB – left-handed batsman
OB – off-break bowler
SLA – slow left arm spin
SRA – slow right arm
RM – right-arm medium pace
RFM – right-arm fast medium
RMF – right-arm medium fast
RF – right-arm fast
LM – left-arm medium pace
LMF – left-arm medium fast
LF – left-arm fast
LB – leg break bowler
WK – wicketkeeper

INTRODUCTION

Choosing the best 100 cricketers to have represented the great county of Yorkshire, with its history of considerable success, was never going to be an easy task. Rather than going for a hit-and-miss affair in which there would be debate over why someone was selected instead of a similar player, we decided that there would be certain criteria that a player had to meet in order to gain entry into this volume. These criteria were as follows: players must have had an appearance in at least 30 first-class matches (as defined by the Association of Cricket Statisticians and Historians) for Yorkshire and done at least one of the following:

Played Test cricket for England during his career with Yorkshire.
Scored 8,000 runs or taken 500 wickets in first-class matches for Yorkshire.
Led the county for at least five seasons or captained a championship-winning side and later served on committee.
Scored the first century, the first double-century or was the first to score 1,000 runs in a season – for Yorkshire in each case.
Taken over 200 wickets in a career for Yorkshire at an average of less than 10.
Kept wicket regularly for Yorkshire for at least five seasons.
Carried his bat through an innings on at least five occasions.
Taken ten wickets in an innings.

Twenty of the players are honoured with a two-page spread. The choice of this group is a personal one made by the authors, and the careers of the cricketers in it stretch from 1866 right up to the present day. It is therefore representative of virtually the entire history of Yorkshire County Cricket Club.

All statistics in this book conform to those published by the ACS and are correct as of 31 March 2001. The term first-class, in this context, includes 'important' matches in the early years which involved some of the players who appear in this book. In the case of some players, the use of ACS first-class match lists means that their figures contradict those published in the *Yorkshire CCC Year Book*; the reason for this is the status of five matches played between 1878 and 1893. The players whose figures are affected by this are indicated by an asterix.

Although the Yorkshire CCC was not formed until January 1863, four players included in this book had already been playing for teams known as Yorkshire. For these cricketers – G. Anderson, R. Iddison, E. Stephenson and J. Thewlis snr – their county career records include games played before 1863 and, therefore, also contradict their figures as published in the *Yorkshire CCC Year Book*.

For three players there are matches in which they appeared where no full bowling analysis is available. The number of wickets taken in these matches is indicated after their wicket total, following a + sign. Thus G. Freeman is shown as 209+4.

BIBLIOGRAPHY

Arnold, P. & Wynne-Thomas, P., *Cricket in Conflict.*
Bailey, P., Thorn, P. and Wynne-Thomas, P., *Who's Who of Cricketers.*
Bartlett, K., *Paul Gibb, His Record, Innings-by-Innings.*
Blakey, R.J., *Taking it from Behind.*
Boothroyd, D., *Half-a-Century of Yorkshire Cricket.*
Bowes, W.E., *Express Deliveries.*
Boycott, G., *The Autobiography.*
Brooke, R., *The Collins Who's Who of English First-Class Cricket; A History of the County Championship.*
Callaghan, J., *Boycott – A Cricketing Legend; Yorkshire's Pride.*
Chesterton, G. & Doggart, H., *Oxford and Cambridge Cricket.*
Clark, C.D., *The Test Match Career of Geoffrey Boycott.*
Close, D.B., *I Don't Bruise Easily.*
Coldham, J.P. *F.S.Jackson; Lord Hawke.*
Duckworth, L., *Holmes and Sutcliffe – The Run Stealers.*
Dyson, P.E., *Benson & Hedges Cup Record Book 1972-1995.*
Frindall, W., *England Test Cricketers; The Wisden Book of Test Cricket; The Wisden Book of Cricket Records; Limited-Overs International Cricket, the Complete Record.*
Gibson, A., *The Cricket Captains of England.*
Green, B. (compiler.), *The Wisden Book of Obituaries.*
Hampshire, J.H., *Family Argument.*
Hatton, L., *Sunday League Record Book 1969-1992.*
Hawke, Lord, *Recollections and Reminiscences.*
Hayter, P. and Botham, I.T., *Botham: My Autobiography.*
Hill, A., *Cricket Conjuror – Johnny Wardle; Hedley Verity – Portrait of a Cricketer; Herbert Sutcliffe – Cricket Maestro.*
Hodgson, D., *The Official History of Yorkshire County Cricket Club.*
Hutton, Sir L., *Cricket is my Life; Fifty Years in Cricket.*
Illingworth, R., *The Tempestuous Years; Yorkshire and Back.*
Isaacs, V. & R., *Gillette Cup & NatWest Trophy Record Book 1963-1996.*
Kilburn, J.M, *A History of Yorkshire Cricket; The History of Yorkshire County Cricket 1924-49.*
Lodge, D., *D.G.Bradman, His Record Innings-by-Innings.*
Martin-Jenkins, C.M.J., *The Wisden Book of County Cricket; World Cricketers; The Complete Who's Who of Test Cricketers.*
Mosey, D., *Boycott; We Don't Play it for Fun.*
Pope, M., *The Laughing Cricketer of Wombwell; Tragic White Roses; The Archive Photograph Series – Yorkshire County Cricket Club.*
Pullin, A.W., *History of Yorkshire County Cricket 1903-1923; Talks with Old Yorkshire Cricketers.*
Roberts, E.L., *Yorkshire's 22 Championships.*
Stevenson, M., *Illingworth – A Biography.*
Storr, D. (ed.), *Ashley Metcalfe Benefit Brochure.*
Thomas, P., *Yorkshire Cricketers 1839-1939.*
Thomson, A.A., *Hirst and Rhodes.*
Trueman, F.S., *Ball of Fire: The Freddie Trueman Story.*
Warner, Sir P., *Cricket Between the Two Wars.*
Watson, W., *Double International.*
Wilkinson, R.D., *Yorkshire County Cricket Club: First-Class Records 1863-1996.*

Wilson, D., *Mad Jack – an Autobiography*.
Woodhouse, A., *A Who's Who of Yorkshire CCC; The History of Yorkshire CCC; Yorkshire Cricketers 1863-1985*.
Woolgar, J., *England's Test Cricketers; England: the Complete One-Day International Record*.
Wynne-Thomas, P., *The Complete History of Cricket Tours; The Hamlyn A-Z of Cricket Records*.
Yardley, N., *Cricket Campaigns*.

The following ACS publications were consulted: *First-Class Match Lists; First-Class Match Score Books; ACS International Year Books*.

Many newspapers were also used, including: *The Times, Sport on Sunday, Yorkshire Evening Press, Yorkshire Post*, as well as various editions of *The Cricket Statistician, The Cricketer, The Newsletter of The Cricket Society, Playfair Cricket Annual, Playfair Cricket Monthly, The White Rose, Wisden Cricketers' Almanack*, and *Yorkshire CCC Year Books*.

ACKNOWLEDGEMENTS

We are most grateful to Tempus Publishing, and especially James Howarth, for bringing this idea of ours, which first saw the light of day about fifteen years ago, to fruition as a finished product. In addition we are grateful to the following:
Peter Wynne-Thomas, archivist, Nottinghamshire CCC; the staff at the central libraries of Leeds and York; James Holliday, Yorkshire CCC; David Baggett, John Brayford, James Greenfield, Andrew Johnson, Eddie Leadbeater, David Musgrave, Ken Utley, Tony Woodhouse and the Wombwell Cricket Lovers' Society for the loan of photographs.

In addition, the following, some of whom are sadly no longer with us, have provided useful information at various times: Les Ames, Paul Gibb Jnr, George Grainger, Gavin Hamilton, Matthew Hoggard, Sir Leonard Hutton, Malcolm Lorimer, Thelma Popple, Nigel Pullan, Phil Staves, E.W. Swanton, Tony Vann, Michael Vaughan and Norman Yardley.

Paul Dyson, Easingwold, York
Mick Pope, Scholes, Rotherham
March 2001

WHO WERE THE GREATEST?

During the latter part of 2000, Yorkshire members took part in a vote to nominate who, in their opinion, was the greatest player in each of eight categories. The result of the vote was:

Opening batsman	Len Hutton
All-rounder	Wilfred Rhodes
Middle-order batsman	Maurice Leyland
Captain	Brian Sellers
Fast bowler	Fred Trueman
Wicketkeeper	Jimmy Binks
Slow/Spin bowler	Hedley Verity
Fielder	Phil Sharpe

Add to these eight Herbert Sutcliffe, Brian Close and George Hirst and we have Yorkshire's team to take on all-comers.

100 Yorkshire Greats

George Anderson
Bob Appleyard
Thomas Armitage
Bill Athey
David Bairstow
Wilf Barber
Billy Bates
Jimmy Binks
Richard Blakey
Major Booth
Bill Bowes
Geoff Boycott
Don Brennan
Jack Brown
Ronnie Burnet
David Byas
Phil Carrick
Brian Close
Geoff Cope
Alec Coxon
David Denton
Arthur Dolphin
Alonzo Drake
Tom Emmett
George Freeman
Paul Gibb
Darren Gough
Andrew Greenwood
Schofield Haigh
Louis Hall
Harry Halliday
Gavin Hamilton
John Hampshire
Peter Hartley
Lord Hawke
Allen Hill
George Hirst
Matthew Hoggard
Percy Holmes
David Hunter
Joseph Hunter
Len Hutton
Richard Hutton
Roger Iddison
Ray Illingworth
Stanley Jackson
Paul Jarvis
Roy Kilner
Eddie Leadbeater
Ted Lester
Maurice Leyland
Ephraim Lockwood
Jim Love
Frank Lowson
Richard Lumb
George Macaulay
Ashley Metcalfe
Frank Milligan
Arthur Mitchell
Frank Mitchell
Martyn Moxon
Tony Nicholson
Chris Old
Edgar Oldroyd
Doug Padgett
Edmund Peate
Bobby Peel
George Pinder
Wilfred Rhodes
Ellis Robinson
Emmott Robinson
Brian Sellers
Kevin Sharp
Phil Sharpe
Arnie Sidebottom
Chris Silverwood
Frank Smailes
Gerald Smithson
Ned Stephenson
Graham Stevenson
Bryan Stott
Herbert Sutcliffe
Ken Taylor
John Thewlis
Fred Trueman
John Tunnicliffe
George Ulyett
Michael Vaughan
Hedley Verity
Abram Waddington
Ted Wainwright
Johnny Wardle
Willie Watson
Craig White
Benjamin Wilson
Don Wilson
Rockley Wilson
Vic Wilson
Arthur Wood
Norman Yardley

The top twenty, who appear here in italics, are each covered on two pages instead of the usual one.

George Anderson

RHB, 1850-1869

Full Name: George Anderson
Birth: Aiskew, Bedale, North Yorkshire 20/01/1826
Death: Bedale, 27/11/1902

Type of Player: Middle order right-hand batsman

First Class Career for Yorkshire:
Debut: XIV of Yorks v All England XI, Hyde Park,Sheffield, 1850
Matches: 33
Batting: 984 runs (Av. 20.50) Highest Score: 99* v Nottinghamshire, Trent Bridge, 1864
Bowling: N/A
Fielding: 29 catches
Year of last match: 1869

Tests: Nil

Such was the progress of George Anderson as a youngster that his first serious game was at the age of sixteen, when he played in a fixture at Sheffield, the opponents' names including a certain W.G. Grace. Having steadily gained a good reputation for his batting, his first game for the All England XI came in the year following his first game for the then 'Yorkshire' team.

Anderson was a very powerful striker of the ball, 'perhaps the hardest hitter that ever played for Yorkshire' according to Reverend R.S. Holmes in 1903, and being six foot tall, took advantage of his height to play from an upright position. As well as power in his strokes there was style too, particularly on the leg side and in front of the wicket. He always played forcing shots to balls on and outside the off-stump and was 'particularly valuable when conditions or circumstances were most difficult'. As far as fielding was concerned, he excelled in the outfield, especially in the deep on the leg side.

1856 saw the highest innings of Anderson's career with Yorkshire, a score of 165 coming in a non-first-class match against the Dalton Club, near Huddersfield. The pinnacle of Anderson's career was in 1862, however, when he became the first player to score 1,000 runs in a season for Yorkshire. The fact that most of these runs came in non-first-class matches is significant but the feat was not repeated for another fourteen years.

His career was marred by a dispute with some Surrey players that had started in a North against South fixture in 1862. The bad feeling festered and, after Yorkshire had excluded Anderson from its fixtures in 1866, an attempt at compromise failed. He was well-respected amongst his fellow-professionals and some other counties were willing to play games against unofficial Yorkshire teams.

Anderson's only foreign tour was in 1863/64 when he was vice-captain on a trip to Australia. He was not seen at his best because of illness and played in only a few games. Following his last match for Yorkshire he played for the All England XI for two more seasons and his final game of any type was when he scored 114 retired for Constable Burton against Darlington at the age of fifty. He received belated recognition for a distinguished career when a benefit match was arranged at Bedale in 1895 which raised a total of £325.

Bob Appleyard

RHB and RM/OB, 1950-1958

Full Name: Robert Appleyard
Birth: Wibsey, Bradford. 27/06/1924

Type of Player: Tail-end right-hand batsman, right-arm medium pace or off-break bowler

First Class Career for Yorkshire:
Debut: v. Scotland, Raeburn Place, Edinburgh, 1950
Matches: 133
Batting: 679 runs (Av. 8.59) Highest Score: 63 v Kent, Tunbridge Wells, 1957
Bowling: 642 wkts (Av. 15.42), 5wi 54 times. Best performance: 8-76 v. MCC, Scarborough, 1951
Fielding: 70 catches
Year of last match: 1958

Tests: 9, 1954-1956

Many judges, including no less a bowling expert than Yorkshire's own Bill Bowes, considered Bob Appleyard one of the best bowlers of all time. But for injury and illness, he might well have gone on to confirm that judgement.

A relative late-comer to first-class cricket, he made his debut for Yorkshire in 1950 at the age of twenty-six, having developed his skills in the Bradford League with Manningham Mills and Bowling Old Lane. In his first full season for the county in 1951, Appleyard became only the fourth player in Yorkshire's history (after Rhodes, Hirst and Macaulay) to take 200 wickets in a season, topping the first-class averages in the process, and was selected as one of *Wisden*'s five in the 1952 edition.
He started out as a right-arm fast-medium in-swing bowler who utilised his full 6 ft 2 in to extract additional bounce, combined with extraordinary accuracy. He worked hard, adding even greater variety to his bowling armoury by perfecting the out-swinger. With encouragement he developed the off-break, making the ball spin faster than normal using his second or middle finger rather than the orthodox first finger. Devasting on wet or sticky wickets, batsmen, even on good pitches, could never feel totally secure against Appleyard's clever variations of pace, seam, guile and spin.

After the tremendous 1951 season, he contracted tuberculosis and missed the next two seasons, before re-emerging in 1954. A tally of 141 wickets, including seven on his Test debut, against Pakistan at Trent Bridge, brought selection in Len Hutton's party for the 1954/55 tour to Australia. There he played a supportive role, taking 11 wickets in 4 Tests, to Tyson and Statham in England's 3-1 Ashes triumph and went on to take 4 for 7 in the second Test against New Zealand at Auckland when the home side slumped to 26 all out. Thereafter, a shoulder injury and further illness restricted his first-class appearances, although in 1956 he captured 110 wickets for Yorkshire and made the last of his 9 Test appearances. He finally retired in 1958 as the wear and tear of professional cricket took an increasing toll. His career record was 708 first-class wickets, at 15.48 apiece.

After the premature close of his playing career, he became a successful businessman, an avid collector of cricket memorabilia and a dedicated committee member for Yorkshire CCC. He was one of the principal workers behind the establishment of the Yorkshire Cricket Academy at his beloved Bradford Park Avenue in 1989.

Thomas Armitage

RHB and RM, 1872-1879

Full Name: Thomas Armitage*
Birth: Walkley, Sheffield. 25/04/1848
Death: Pullman, Chicago, USA, 21/09/1922

Type of Player: Opening/middle order right-hand batsman, right-arm medium pace or underhand lob bowler

First Class Career for Yorkshire:
Debut: v. Nottinghamshire, Trent Bridge, 1872
Matches: 52
Batting: 1053 runs (Av. 13.85) Highest Score: 95 v Middlesex, Bramall Lane, Sheffield, 1876
Bowling: 106 wkts (Av. 15.05), 5wi 10 times. Best performance: 7-26 v. Surrey, Bramall Lane, Sheffield, 1876
Fielding: 20 catches
Year of last match: 1879

Tests: 2, 1876/77

A useful cricketer with a somewhat 'bulky and robust' physique, Sheffield's Tom Armitage stood, according to *Scores & Biographies*, 5 ft 10 1/2 in and weighed in at 12 st 10 lb. He put that powerful frame to good use for Yorkshire in the 1870s. By trade he was a mason, but cricket was his pleasure and he was engaged as a professional cricketer, firstly with the Longsight club in Manchester and then Keighley from 1870 to 1875. In 1872 he took 18 wickets in a match against Wakefield, including all ten in the opposition's second innings.

Although it was 1872 when Armitage first appeared for Yorkshire, it wasn't until 1875 that his performances became worthy of note. His powerful batting was always sound and that season his highest score was 68 not out against Surrey. The following summer he made his highest first-class score at Bramall Lane. Above all else though, it was his cunning lob bowling that firmly established him in the Yorkshire ranks. He took 5 for 8 against Nottinghamshire at Trent Bridge in 1875, and that same season bowled unchanged throughout both completed innings with Allen Hill for a United North of England XI against a Derbyshire XI, capturing 12 for 61 in the match. A year later his match figures of 13 for 46 against Surrey at Bramall Lane caused *Wisden* to comment that they had never 'seen lobs that were so good'.

Such success brought Armitage inclusion in James Lillywhite's 1876/77 tour party to Australia alongside four other county colleagues: Greenwood, Hill, Emmett and Ulyett. Australia beat England by 45 runs in the historic first ever 'Test Match' and for Armitage it was not a successful venture. *Wisden* later commented that: 'He was a failure in Australia, falling far below his form at home.' In the two Tests he had scores of just 9, 3 and 21 and bowled only 3 overs in the two matches at a cost of 15 runs. Still, his high floating lobs caused one Australian to comment that 'you needed a clothes prop to play 'em!'

His portly figure caused constant comment, none more typical than that from his Yorkshire colleague Tom Emmett, who likened the slender opening batsman Louis Hall and Armitage to 'Law and Gospel', and when asked for an explanation, replied, 'Shadow and Substance'.

After his Yorkshire playing days were over he emigrated to America, where he coached and became groundsman at Pullman Cricket Club, Chicago. He stayed there until his death, outliving all but one – James Lillywhite jnr – of England's first Test XI.

Bill Athey

RHB and OB, 1976-1983

Full Name: Charles William Jeffrey Athey
Birth: Middlesbrough. 27/09/1957

Type of Player: Opening middle order right-hand batsman, off-break bowler.

First Class Career for Yorkshire:
Debut: v. Cambridge University, Fenner's, 1976
Matches: 151
Batting: 6320 runs (Av. 28.08), 10 centuries.
Highest Score: 134 v Derbyshire, Derby 1982
Bowling: 21 wkts (Av. 47.76) Best performance: 3-38 v. Surrey, The Oval, 1978
Fielding: 144 catches, 2 stumpings
Year of last match: 1983

Tests: 23, 1980-1988

One of the most promising batsmen of his era, Bill Athey, disappointingly, never quite fulfilled his potential with the county side. A product of Acklam Hall High School, his classical technique was extremely well-founded and he scored his maiden first-class century as early as his ninth innings. However, he never seemed certain as to whether to play his natural stroke-playing game or follow the example of Boycott and concentrate on wearing the bowlers down with watchful defence. The latter seemed to be the dominant style and it was certainly used to England's advantage during his Test career.

Athey received his county cap in 1980 and his best season for Yorkshire was in 1982, when he scored four centuries, so it was something of a blow when he left the county at the end of the following season. He was widely seen as the natural successor to Boycott, but it was widely assumed that his departure had much to do with the troubles that surrounded that same player and which Athey may have realised were approaching their peak.

The pinnacle of his career was the 1986/87 season in Australia when he was an integral part of an Ashes-winning team under Mike Gatting. He batted throughout the first day of the First Test at Brisbane and forged a most effective opening partnership with Chris Broad, their stands including one of 223 at Perth. Athey's only Test century, 123 against Pakistan, was during the following summer but a successful England team soon broke up. His limited-overs international career consisted of 31 matches and included two centuries.

Athey's second county was Gloucestershire and the best season of his career (1,812 runs, average 37.75) was his first with them. His highest first-class score, 184 for England 'B' against Sri Lanka at Galle, came during a period of consistent run-making. He captained his new county in 1989 but moved to Sussex for the 1993 season. He was coach at Worcestershire from 1998, until his resignation after a disappointing 2000 season.

A career that produced 25,453 first-class runs and 11,915 in limited-overs matches – including 3,653 for his native county – would be seen as highly productive by many. However, there is a niggling feeling that with better man-management by both his original county and his country he could have been more than just 'a young batsman who possesses the talent to adorn the England side for many years to come', as M.H. Stevenson said of him in 1980.

David Bairstow

RHB , WK and RM, 1970-1990

Full Name: David Leslie Bairstow
Birth: Bradford. 01/09/1951
Death: Marton-cum-Grafton, Boroughbridge, 05/01/1998

Type of Player: Lower middle order right-hand batsman, wicketkeeper, right-arm medium pace bowler

First Class Career for Yorkshire:
Debut: v. Gloucestershire, Bradford, 1970
Matches: 429
Batting: 12,985 runs (Av. 26.60), 9 centuries. Highest Score: 45 v.Middlesex, Scarborough, 1980
Bowling: 6 wkts (Av. 32.00) Best performance: 3-25 v. MCC, Scarborough, 1987
Fielding: 907 catches, 131 stumpings
Year of last match: 1990

Tests: 4, 1979-1980/81

Beyond question, David 'Bluey' Bairstow was the most popular Yorkshire cricketer of his generation. A stocky red-haired wicketkeeper batsman, he was tough and uncompromising, a man who undoubtedly wore his heart on his sleeve – and that heart was full of Yorkshire cricket.

He began his cricket career at his father's club, Laisterdyke, as a nine-year-old bowler. At fourteen he moved to Undercliffe, in the Bradford League. He was eighteen when Yorkshire called him up to make his county debut. In order to do so, the young Bairstow sat his English A-level paper at Hanson Grammar School at 7.00 a.m. that morning! Whilst the exam was failed, he took comfort from four first innings catches on debut and was set to become the county's regular wicketkeeper for the next twenty years.

As a wicketkeeper he was brisk and noisily efficient behind the stumps, particularly when taking off the faster bowlers. As a catcher of the ball, at full stretch he was without equal among the 'keepers of the day and was unfortunate to be a contemporary of Alan Knott and Bob Taylor. In the Roses match at Manchester in 1971, he took nine catches in the match, including six in the first innings, to equal the previous Yorkshire record held jointly then by Joe Hunter (1887) and Dolphin (1919).

Awarded his county cap in 1973, he had to wait a further six years before making his England Test debut at The Oval against India. An innings of 59 and three catches were rewarded with a tour place to Australia in the winter of 1979/80, although he didn't add to his one Test cap until the Fifth Test against West Indies at Headingley the following summer, when he also played for England in the Centenary Test against Australia at Lord's. Four Test caps in total, the last against West Indies at Bridgetown on the 1980/81 tour of the Caribbean, was perhaps a reasonable return, although in modern times, with the emphasis very much on separate one-day and Test squads, he would have expected to have appeared in many more than his 21 one-day internationals.

His batting steadily improved for Yorkshire and he became an unyielding and aggressive middle-order batsman with a resolute spirit that was never more aptly demonstrated than in the Benson & Hedges

David Bairstow batting for Yorkshire at Scarborough in 1985.

Cup tie against Derbyshire in 1981. Yorkshire were 64 for 5 when Bairstow strode to the wicket. They continued to lose wickets, and when the last man Mark Johnson came in, 80 runs were still needed for an unlikely victory. Bairstow, though, had other ideas and went on the attack. When the winning run was hit – with 8 balls to spare – he had plundered 103 including 9 sixes and 3 fours, his second 50 taking only 17 minutes.

In 1982, when he enjoyed a well-earned benefit which yielded £56,913, he equalled the world record of 11 catches in a match against Derbyshire at Scarborough. A year later he was part of the Yorkshire side that won the Sunday League title under Illingworth's captaincy.

Above all else though, he cherished the captaincy of Yorkshire, which became his in 1984, in the immediate aftermath of the pro-Boycott revolution. The county needed unity and Bairstow's popularity, both inside and outside the dressing room, was seen by the committee as vital to that cause. He led a poor side for three seasons in the same manner in which he played cricket – from the front, with an intensity of pride and a blind loyalty to Yorkshire. The nearest he came to honours was in his first summer as skipper when Warwickshire won a dramatic Benson & Hedges semi-final clash at Headingley by 3 runs after Bairstow himself was brilliantly caught on the cover boundary by Paul Smith, just when he seemed destined to lead the White Rose county to Lord's. That was left to his successor, Carrick, who took up the reigns in 1987 and led Yorkshire to a breathtaking Benson & Hedges triumph over Northamptonshire in his first season in charge.

His county career ended sadly in acrimony in 1990 when the then cricket chairman, Brian Close, broke the news of his release by Yorkshire. By then he had been dropped from the first team in his Testimonial year (which produced £73,997). His 1,038 first-class dismissals for Yorkshire places him third in the club's all-time list behind David Hunter and Binks, who between them cannot match Bairstow's aggregate of nearly 13,000 runs. Added to that statistic is his limited overs record for the county of 5,114 runs, and a further 389 catches and 31 stumpings.

He returned to play cricket for his club side Undercliffe when his first-class career ended and did some commentary work on Radio Five as well as running a sportswear business. News of his tragic suicide at the family home in January 1998 shocked many in the game. A memorial service, attended by 300 mourners, took place at Ripon Cathedral in late February 1998.

David Bairstow will be forever remembered, not only as one of Yorkshire's greatest, but also as one of cricket's most colourful and energetic characters. There were no half measures in the way he lived his life or played the game.

Wilf Barber

RHB and RFM, 1926-1947

Full Name: Wilfred Barber
Birth: Cleckheaton, 18/04/1901
Death: Bradford, 10/09/1968

Type of Player: Opening/middle order right-hand batsman, right-arm fast medium bowler

First Class Career for Yorkshire:
Debut: v. Worcestershire, Bradford, 1926
Matches: 354
Batting: 15,315 runs (Av. 34.26), 27 centuries. Highest Score: 255 v. Surrey, Bramall Lane, Sheffield, 1935
Bowling: 14 wkts (Av.28.85) Best performance: 2-1 v. Worcestershire, Bradford, 1934
Fielding: 169 catches
Year of last match: 1947

Tests: 2, 1935

A pillar of the Yorkshire ranks in the 1930s, Wilf Barber was a member of a very strong batting side that helped the county to dominate the County Championship during the decade. When heavy Test calls deprived Yorkshire of perhaps three players at a time, Barber's true value to the side was demonstrated, as a tenacious middle-order batsman 'with an attractive style' and as an excellent outfielder.

Raised in Gomersal, he became a member of the local club as a boy and, in 1921, top scored for them in the Heavy Woollen Cup final. A late developer in first-class cricket terms, he didn't play for the Yorkshire Second XI until he was twenty-five, and he was unable to gain a regular position in the county first team until 1932. That summer he shared a second-wicket partnership of 346 with Maurice Leyland (189) against Middlesex at Sheffield, which remains a county second-wicket record, his own contribution being 162. Bowes, in his own appreciation of Barber in the *Yorkshire Evening Post*, wrote: 'Perhaps even more than Sir Leonard Hutton, he [Barber] was a text-book player.' Certainly he combined all the right facets of batsmanship – a strong off-side player, he could be patient and able to defend when the situation demanded, but was also capable of fine attacking stroke-play. On eight occasions he scored more than 1,000 runs in a season – with his best 2,147 in 1935 at an average of 42.09, when he also recorded his highest first-class score.

His 2 Test caps were also achieved in that successful summer of 1935. He was one of six Yorkshire cricketers to represent England in the series against South Africa. He made his top score (44) in his second Test at Old Trafford in July and although he toured New Zealand and Australia with the MCC in 1935/36, that was also destined to be his last Test innings.

After the war, he continued to serve Yorkshire until 1947, enjoying a joint testimonial with Cyril Turner in 1946, Barber's share being £2,958. After retiring he became a coach with the North Riding Education Authority and later Ashville College, Harrogate. His service to Yorkshire was unselfish. The doyen of Yorkshire cricket writers, J.M. Kilburn, summed up Barber thus: 'a handsome batsman, small in stature but upright in style with a liking for the off-drive. He was happier in the routine situation than crisis and he preferred the trustworthy pitch to the turning ball but in his own unassertive way he fitted neatly into Yorkshire's pattern.'

Billy Bates

RHB and OB, 1877-1887

Full Name: Willie Bates (known as Billy)
Birth: Lascelles Hall, Huddersfield. 19/11/1855
Death: Lepton, 08/01/1900

Type of Player: Middle order right-hand batsman, off-break bowler

First Class Career for Yorkshire:
Debut: v. Middlesex, Lord's, 1877
Matches: 202
Batting: 6499 runs (Av. 20.37), 8 centuries
Highest Score: 136 v. Sussex, Hove, 1886
Bowling: 637 wkts (Av. 16.78) 5wi 36 times.
Best performance: 8-21 v. Surrey, The Oval, 1879
Fielding: 163 catches
Year of last match: 1887

Tests: 15, 1881/82-1886/87

Melbourne was the venue, 20 January 1883 was the date and this was the setting for Test cricket's first hat-trick by an England player. It was only the eleventh such game; it was also the first time any team had won by an innings and McDonnell, Giffen and Bonnor provided Billy Bates with a distinguished trio of victims. His figures of 7 for 28 were followed up with 7 for 74 in the second innings and a knock of 55 meant that he had become the first player to score a half-century and take ten wickets in a Test – a feat since repeated by only fifteen players world-wide, including just four Englishmen.

On a subsequent visit to Melbourne, five years later, he was not so fortunate; a stray ball during net practice hit him in the eye and this singular act of misfortune brought his distinguished career at first-class level to a sudden end. Cricket had been his life and the resultant depression caused an attempt at suicide. Without an alternative source of income, Bates struggled through the rest of his short life, which included some club cricket and coaching in South Africa. A cold caught at the funeral of J. Thewlis developed into something more serious and his death occurred shortly afterwards. His name lived on, however, through his son W.E. Bates (Yorkshire and Glamorgan) and his grandson Ted Bates, who played for and later managed Southampton FC.

The Lascelles Hall club produced many county players in Bates' time and he first developed as a hard-hitting and fast-scoring batsman, later being most successful on fast pitches. His bowling had great accuracy and flight and he was very popular with the crowds, especially in Australia, which he visited five times. A mounted emu egg, now in the possession of his descendants, was presented to him following a collection on the occasion of his hat-trick.

Although his fielding let him down, Bates was otherwise a complete all-rounder, one of the best of his era. Some 10,249 runs and 874 wickets were the products of his first-class career and his Test career had a similar balance in its 656 runs and 50 wickets. In a period when professionals were not noted for impeccable standards of dress, Bates was always immaculately turned out and earned for himself the nickname of 'The Duke'. This colourful character also provided rich entertainment for the king of the Sandwich Islands with his singing.

Jimmy Binks

RHB, WK and LB, 1955-1969

Full Name: James Graham Binks
Birth: Hull, 05/10/1935

Type of Player: Lower order right-hand batsman, wicketkeeper, leg-break bowler

First Class Career for Yorkshire:
Debut: v. Hampshire, Bournemouth, 1955
Matches: 491
Batting: 6,745 runs (Av. 14.69) Highest Score: 95 v. Middlesex, Lord's, 1964
Bowling: 0 wkts
Wicket-keeping: 872 catches, 172 stumpings
Year of last match: 1969

Tests: 2, 1963/64

Only a very few cricketers emerge from the Hull district, but when they discovered the talents of Jimmy Binks, they unearthed a real gem. He was a brilliantly consistent wicketkeeper and his feat of playing in no less than 412 consecutive County Championship games from his debut until his retirement is a record surely destined to remain.

Binks made his county debut as a nineteen-year-old after an injury to Roy Booth, and he never looked back. The demands placed on him because of the different skills of the Yorkshire bowlers were varied in the extreme but he responded to each with enormous skill and dexterity. He stood back to the high pace of Trueman, gathering the ball with effortless timing and, remarkably, stood up to the wicket for the fast-medium of Platt and, later, Nicholson. The two different styles of Wardle were dealt with equally effectively, as was the contrasting direction of spin forthcoming from Illingworth and Don Wilson.

There was no apparent weakness in Binks' armoury and he gathered the ball with the minimum of fuss and movement. So skillful was he that he suffered only one injury during his entire career – a broken finger in 1966 – but, as with many 'keepers, he played through the discomfort this caused.

It was a bone of contention with Yorkshire supporters that two Tests were scant reward for being regarded as the best 'keeper in the country for so many seasons. When the chance came along Binks seized it but he wasn't expecting the occasion to be remembered for his batting. Pressed into opening the batting because of team illness in India, he scored a half-century and posted a century opening stand with Brian Bolus. Binks' competitor – Jim Parks – played merely as a batsman but it was the Tyke who lost his place when a fuller squad was available for selection.

Binks' best season was 1960, when he totalled 107 dismissals – a county record; the 96 catches also remain as a national record. His well-deserved benefit netted £6,093 in 1967 and he was one of the *Wisden* five for 1969. Despite his lack of international appearances, he took great comfort from being part of a team that won seven Championship titles and two Gillette Cup finals. Throughout, he was the hub of a fine fielding side, his boyish looks combining effectively with his permanent eagerness.

Richard Blakey

RHB and WK, 1985-present

Full Name: Richard John Blakey
Birth: Huddersfield, 15/01/1967

Type of Player: Middle order right-hand batsman, wicketkeeper

First Class Career for Yorkshire:
Debut: v. Middlesex, Headingley, 1985
Matches: 295
Batting: 12,236 runs (Av. 30.36), 10 centuries
Highest Score: 204* v. Gloucestershire, Headingley, 1987
Bowling: 1wkt (Av. 68.00) Best performance: 1-68 v. Nottinghamshire., Abbeydale Park, Sheffield,1986
Wicketkeeping: 658 catches, 49 stumpings

Tests: 2, 1992/93

The 1991 season was the turning point in the career of Richard Blakey. He had been an extremely promising batsman with a niche in the top three of the order. Soon, however, in the interests of Yorkshire cricket, he became a wicketkeeper-batsman and his position in the order became lower and lower. Blakey broke into the Yorkshire side as an eighteen-year-old, after attending Rastrick Grammar School, and soon showed that he was a player with a good technique and scoring strokes on both sides of the wicket. Two years after his debut he was in the team which won the Benson & Hedges Cup and he topped a memorable season by becoming the youngest player to score a double century for Yorkshire, and received his county cap. At the end of the season, which remains his best in terms of runs (1,361, average 41.42), he was elected Young Cricketer of the Year.

The highest innings of Blakey's career was a marathon 221 for England 'A' against Zimbabwe at Bulawayo in 1989/90. *Wisden* commented that the player 'showed the temperament and remorseless concentration required for five-day cricket'. Lasting almost ten hours it was, at the time, the second-longest innings ever played in Africa. Three years later Blakey's only full England trip was not so successful. His four innings at the highest level produced only seven runs as the Indian spinners tormented him.

Although his 'keeping improved enough for him to top the national list with 71 victims in 1998 – his benefit season which earned £122,438 – his batting opportunities became more limited. Being sent in as low as number nine during the 1999 season was inappropriate for an experienced player and, when others failed, Blakey's response to promotion was to score his first century for three years. Unfortunately the runs dried up during 2000 and he ended up being dropped from the Championship side. Although he retained his place in the one-day side, his position at the club appears to be no longer secure.

In limited-overs matches, where possibly Blakey's batting skills have been at their most efficient, he now has a run-tally of 6,368 (av 32.66) and he also has 277 catches and 39 stumpings to his credit. Consistency has been a feature of Blakey's 'keeping over the years for Yorkshire; he did not miss a Championship match from August 1992 to August 2000 and although he may look laid-back, the injuries which he has overcome and played through prove that his dedication is real.

Major Booth

RHB and RMF, 1908-1914

Full Name: Major William Booth
Birth: Lowtown, Pudsey, 10/12/1886
Death: La Cigny, Serre, France, 01/07/1916

Type of Player: Middle/ lower order right-hand batsman, right-arm medium fast bowler

First Class Career for Yorkshire:
Debut: v. Somerset, Dewsbury, 1908
Matches: 144
Batting: 4,244 runs (Av. 22.69), 2 centuries.
Highest Score: 210 v. Worcestershire, Worcester, 1911
Bowling: 557 wkts (Av. 19.17), 5wi 41 times.
Best performance: 8-47 v. Middlesex, Headingley, 1912
Fielding: 114 catches
Year of last match: 1914

Tests: 2, 1913/14

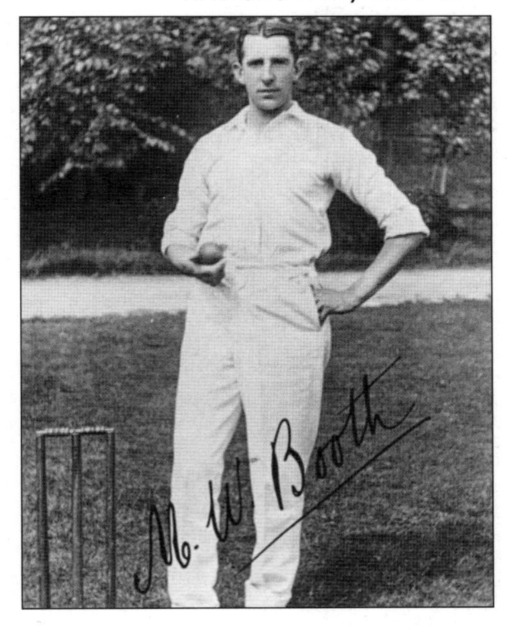

The period between 1914 and 1919 robbed Yorkshire cricket of two of its finest all-round prospects. Drake was one, the other was Major William Booth. A fine punishing batsman, Booth was also a tall, medium fast bowler who was in his prime as a cricketer when the First World War broke out.

Born in Pudsey, West Yorkshire, he schooled at Fulneck, and although he lived close to the Pudsey Britannia ground he played his early cricket with Pudsey St Lawrence. He moved to Wath CC in the winter of 1908/09 when working at a local colliery in South Yorkshire. He had already represented Yorkshire at first-class level, although it took him a further two years to cement a regular place. His batting first grabbed headlines in 1911, with a double century at Worcester, prompting one Yorkshire journalist to comment: 'the ease with which he made his runs was astonishing. Few finer examples of off-driving and square cutting can have been seen.' As a bowler he possessed a free, natural action and his height enabled him to extract considerable bounce, as many county sides found to their cost, particularly in the three seasons immediately before the war when he captured over 100 wickets per summer.

His best return for Yorkshire came in 1913 with 167 wickets; 181 in all first-class matches and 1,228 runs ensured the 'double' and a place on the MCC tour of South Africa that winter. England, whose bowling was led by S.F. Barnes (49 wickets in four Tests), won the rubber 4-0. Booth played in the First Test at Durban and the Fifth at Port Elizabeth, scoring 46 runs and taking 7 wickets in the two matches. He returned home to find himself one of *Wisden*'s Five Cricketers of the Year in the 1914 edition. Later in the 1914 season, he formed a deadly combination with county bowling colleague, Drake. Together they bowled unchanged against Gloucestershire at Bristol (Booth's match figures being 12 for 89), and against Somerset at Weston-super-Mare where Booth played a supporting role (5 for 77 in the match) to Drake who was Yorkshire's first bowler to capture all ten wickets in an innings. By the premature close to the season due to the war, Booth had 157 first-class wickets at an average of 17.85.

Major Booth was killed in action while serving as a Second Lieutenant in the West Yorkshire Regiment in France, having joined up alongside his fellow Yorkshire colleagues Dolphin and Roy Kilner. Yorkshire's proud President Lord Hawke summed up the county's loss: 'England lost one of the most promising and charming young cricketers it was ever my lot to meet.'

Bill Bowes

RHB and RMF, 1929-1947

Full Name: William Eric Bowes
Birth: Elland, 25/07/1908
Death: Otley, 04/09/1987

Type of Player: Tail-end right-hand batsman, right-arm medium fast bowler

First Class Career for Yorkshire:
Debut: v. Essex, Leyton, 1929
Matches: 301
Batting: 1,251 runs (Av. 8.93) Highest Score: 43* v. Gloucestershire, Scarborough, 1938
Bowling: 1,351 wkts (Av. 15.71), 5wi 103 times. Best performance: 9-121 v. Essex, Scarborough, 1932
Fielding: 108 catches
Year of last match: 1947

Tests: 15, 1932-1946

In the 1930s Yorkshire won the County Championship seven times; in that same decade Bill Bowes only once was below tenth place in the national bowling averages. These two facts are inextricably linked, for Bowes was the leader of the team's pace attack during that decade, being one of the most effective swing bowlers the county have ever produced.

A hat-trick for West Leeds High School and successful league cricket encouraged him to take up the suggestion that he write to Lord's for a trial. The success of this, in January 1928, meant that he was able to make his first-class debut for MCC against Wales later the same year. Another hat-trick, against Cambridge University at Lord's, was well-timed and Yorkshire were alerted to his progress. The county and the MCC agreed to a compromise – Bowes would be free to play for Yorkshire when not required by Lord's.

During this period of learning he found how to bowl with variation both of pace and movement. His height (6 ft 5 in) was an advantage and he gained considerable bounce and real pace on the hard pitches of the time. His natural ball was the in-swinger but the ball moving in the opposite direction was soon added to his armoury, which included a well-disguised yorker; this led to the attentions of the Test selectors as well as him being named as one of the *Wisden* five for the 1932 edition.

Bowes' England debut included his first experience of the uncompromising and original captaincy of Douglas Jardine. Bowes and Bill Voce were asked by Jardine to bowl at least one full toss per over in the second innings, the theory being that the ball was difficult to see because the pavilion end had no sight-screen then. Neither bowler complied and were admonished only lightly afterwards, as Jardine's team had easily beaten India and he was pleased with his first Test as leader.

Later in the same season, playing against Surrey at The Oval, Bowes took part in a match 'which marked the start of the great bodyline controversy'. He bowled an occasional bouncer to Jack Hobbs and when some of the Yorkshire players felt that the batsman was discomforted, this encouraged Bowes to bowl more. The on-side field became strengthened and this set Jardine, another batsman involved, thinking.

For the following winter, Bowes was in the MCC party which had set out to recover the Ashes. In an early game he was bowling in a hostile manner with a series of bouncers; when he asked for an extra man on the on-side, Jardine declined, stating that he could have five more but not one. Bowes didn't want five so was taken off. The two men reached an understanding later but Bowes played in only one of the five infamous Tests. One wicket was his reward but at least it was that of Bradman – the player for whom bodyline was reputedly devised – for a duck, playing on to a ball which he expected to bounce higher. Bowes' feelings on the whole episode were supportive towards Jardine's policy. Writing later, he stated, 'leg theory ... came as a natural evolution of the game. There was nothing sinister about it, and nothing sinister was intended.'

The number of Tests in which Bowes played was scant reward for his efficiency and consistency as a bowler. However much his limited batting and fielding disadvantaged him, his return of 68 wickets (average 22.33) justified his appearances. He took five wickets in an innings six times, his best being six for 33 against the West Indies at Old Trafford in 1939. Bowes's best county figures were on a hot day on a batsman's wicket; he persevered for 40 overs in three-and-a-half hours. In the wetter summer of 1935 he took advantage of alternative conditions. Forty wickets for 321 runs in four consecutive games contributed to his best season in terms of aggregate, his tally of 193 wickets (average 15.44) coming in all first-class matches. A slightly better average (15.23) occurred when he topped the national averages for the only time, in 1938, with 121 victims.

During the Second World War he lost over four stones, spending more than two years in prison camps and he was never the same again. He was rewarded with a benefit of £8,083 in 1947 and soon began a second career in the game – as a journalist. He became cricket correspondent for the *Yorkshire Evening News* and, later, for the *Evening Post*. His kindly disposition was well respected by everyone who came into contact with him.

Australian captain Bill Woodfull bowled by Bill Bowes during the Oval Test of 1934.

Bowes retired from full-time writing in 1973. He was an unlikely-looking cricketer, being unathlectic and bespectacled. Yet a full career record of 1,639 wickets and an average of 16.76 speaks volumes about his intelligent and thorough approach to the game. He remains one of the very few players to have taken more wickets than scored runs in a first-class career, a fact which appealed to his dry sense of humour.

Geoff Boycott

RHB and RM, 1962-1986

Full Name: Geoffrey Boycott, OBE
Birth: Fitzwilliam, Pontefract, 21/10/1940

Type of Player: Opening right-hand batsman, right-arm medium pace bowler

First Class Career for Yorkshire:
Debut: v. Pakistanis, Bradford, 1962
Matches: 414
Batting: 32,570 runs (Av. 57.85), 103 centuries. Highest Score: 260* v. Essex, Colchester, 1970
Bowling: 28 wkts (Av. 23.75) Best performance: 4-14 v. Lancashire, Headingley, 1979
Fielding: 200 catches
Year of last match: 1986

Tests: 108, 1964-1981/82

Dedicated to run-making almost in the extreme, Geoff Boycott reached the pinnacle of his career on 23 December 1981, at Delhi, when he became the highest-scoring Test batsman. The following Test was the last of his 108, he departed the scene in controversial circumstances and his 8,114-run record (average 47.72) stood for just 690 days. Boycott excelled at Hemsworth Grammar School and played for Ackworth and Barnsley in his teens. Three centuries in his first full season (1963), including two in his first matches against Lancashire, contributed to him being awarded his county cap and being elected Young Cricketer of the Year and one of the *Wisden* five for 1964.

Boycott's wicket soon became prized on the county and Test circuit. He was regarded as a batsman with a defensive technique approaching perfection; his favourite attacking stroke was the square cut but he scored runs all round the wicket even employing the hook stroke, which he was to cut from his repertoire later in his career. It was a surprise, therefore, when 1965 was a disappointment and his first-class matches did not produce a century. The shackles were removed, especially for a cup final crowd at Lord's when he scored a brilliantly attacking 146 to take the Man of the Match award and provide the telling contribution in a Yorkshire victory. Boycott's highest Test score, 246 not out against India at Headingley in 1967, resulted in him being dropped for the next Test. His 108 on the first day was too slow for the selectors.

The following season he topped the national averages for the first of six occasions, including three in a row from 1971 to 1973, and he reached his peak in world standings when England recovered the Ashes in 1970/71. These Tests produced 657 runs (average 93.85), and was Boycott's best series. During that winter Boycott was appointed captain of Yorkshire and he led them for eight seasons without any tangible success. His immediate response was to produce his best aggregate (2,503) and become the first Englishman to average over 100 in a season. Second place in the Championship in 1975 proved a false dawn and the responsibility of being the team's best batsman started to weigh heavily.

Boycott began to score more slowly and an incident at Northampton when John Hampshire followed suit was a definite factor in him being sacked at the end of the 1978 season. That the committee could not wait to wield the axe was proved by the fact that he was tactlessly informed of the decision just two days after the death of his mother.

Meanwhile, following the granting of the England captaincy to Mike Denness and failures against India's innocuous bowlers, he began a period of self-imposed exile from the Test scene. When he returned in 1977 he crowned his comeback with his 100th first-class century, in the Headingley Test against Australia, reached amid scenes of great jubilation.

In the following winter he led England, for the first and only time, in four Tests in Pakistan and New Zealand. Boycott averaged over 100 again in 1979 and in the following winter, in Australia, he batted brilliantly in the one-day internationals against the feared pace attack of the home side and West Indies. He scored one century and received two match awards, top-scoring in five out of the six games he played. The next winter he faced, from Michael Holding, two of the fastest overs ever bowled and scores of 0 and 1 at the age of thirty-eight might have signalled the end for many players.

Matters were boiling up in Yorkshire and the early 1980s saw a series of public clashes between Boycott and manager Illingworth. When Boycott was sacked at the end of 1983 but given a testimonial for 1984 the membership got involved to the tune of expressing motions of no confidence in the General and Cricket Committees and electing fresh faces onto the scene. Boycott's testimonial produced £147,954 (to add to his 1974 benefit of £20,639 – both records) and he was able to play on for three more seasons before the curtain was finally drawn. Boycott has since worked energetically for the media; his radio and television comments have been lively and apposite, although he tends to discuss his own past and avoid discretion at times.

Geoff Boycott batting for England against the Rest of the World team, August 1970.

Boycott's first-class tally of 48,426 runs (the eighth highest) was made at an average of 56.83 and this is the best amongst the 61 who have passed 30,000. His highest first-class score was 261 not out in a tour game at Bridgetown in 1973/74. His 8,481 runs (average 39.63) in limited-overs matches are a record for Yorkshire. Contrast this with his apparent lack of personal supporters from his cricketing contemporaries and there stands one of the greatest paradoxes of Yorkshire cricket.

Don Brennan

RHB and WK, 1947-1953

Full Name: Donald Vincent Brennan
Birth: Eccleshill, Bradford, 10/02/1920
Death: Ilkley, 09/01/1985

Type of Player: Lower order right-hand batsman, wicketkeeper

First Class Career for Yorkshire:
Debut: v. MCC, Lord's, 1947
Matches: 204
Batting: 1,653 runs (Av. 10.66) Highest Score: 47 v. Middlesex, Bradford, 1951
Bowling: n/a
Wicketkeeping: 280 catches, 100 stumpings
Year of last match: 1953

Tests: 2, 1951

Remembered for his white wicketkeeping gauntlets, Don Brennan was the first amateur ever to keep wicket regularly for Yorkshire. His opportunity came after Paul Gibb turned professional and moved to Essex, allowing Brennan to become the county's 'keeper from 1947 to 1953.

Originally a fast bowler educated at Downside school, he played cricket for the Army in Egypt during the war, developing into a stylish wicketkeeper. Tall and slim, he was highly regarded by the professionals in the side, especially for his work standing up to the wicket, which was often the case with the likes of Wardle, Appleyard and Leadbeater in the Yorkshire XI. His work down the leg-side was often outstanding. Fellow colleague Billy Sutcliffe, writing in tribute of Brennan's ability in 1986, wrote: 'I have never seen a better 'keeper standing up on a sticky wicket. Standing back was not enough of a challenge for Don.' He was good enough to keep Godfrey Evans out of the England side for a brief spell in 1951 when he won his two Test caps against South Africa, making his debut alongside Peter May and county team-mate Lowson at Headingley. He had just 16 runs and one stumping to add to his career tally from those two Test appearances. Had his career not clashed with that of Evans he might well have played more times for his country.

He did tour India, Pakistan and Ceylon in 1951/52 and made his only first-class half century (67 not out) against Maharashtra in India on the trip. As a batsman he was a 'dogged defender', and for Yorkshire his best moments with the bat came against Worcestershire in August 1948 when he and Sellers added 106 for the tenth wicket (Brennan 30 not out) and when he made a score of 47 against Middlesex at Park Avenue three years later.

The requirements of the family textile business brought a somewhat early retirement from the game in 1953; his 204 matches had yielded just over 1,600 runs and 380 dismissals and for several seasons he was considered as Norman Yardley's unofficial vice-captain on the field. He served on the Yorkshire committee from 1971 until illness prevented this in 1984. He was devoted to Yorkshire cricket and, while he may have appeared outspoken during his committee days, his prime concern remained what he considered to be the welfare of Yorkshire cricket above all else. Despite the relative shortness of his career it is doubtful if a more gifted or natural wicketkeeper has ever represented the county.

Jack Brown

RHB and LB, 1889-1904

Full Name: John Thomas Brown
Birth: Driffield, 20/08/1869
Death: Pimlico, Westminster, London, 04/11/1904

Type of Player: Opening right-hand batsman, right-arm leg-break bowler

First Class Career for Yorkshire:
Debut: v. Gloucestershire, Bradford, 1889
Matches: 346
Batting: 15,762 runs (Av. 29.90), 23 centuries
Highest Score: 311 v. Sussex, Bramall Lane, Sheffield, 1897
Bowling: 177 wkts (Av. 29.28), 5wi 4 times. Best performance: 6-52 v. Sussex, Bradford, 1898
Fielding: 189 catches
Year of last match: 1904

Tests: 8, 1894/95-1899

Alongside Tunnicliffe, J.T. Brown, as he was widely known, formed an opening partnership rivalled in Yorkshire's history only by that of Holmes and Sutcliffe in the 1920s and '30s. A short, neat and stylish batsman from Driffield, Brown was only nineteen when he first played for Yorkshire, but illness prevented him from making an impact until 1894, when he passed 1,000 runs for the first of ten successive seasons. That form won him a place in the team to Australia in 1894/95 following the withdrawal of Abel and selection amongst *Wisden*'s 1895 'Five Young Batsmen of the Season'. He was an outstanding success on the tour, topping the English Test averages with 343 runs, including a sensational innings of 140 in the Fifth Test at Melbourne – his first 50 took just 28 minutes. That thrilling knock was his solitary Test hundred and he played only three further times for his country. With Tunnicliffe, the pair recorded 19 century opening partnerships for Yorkshire including 378 against Sussex at Sheffield in 1897 (Brown 311) and a year later a new world-record first-wicket stand of 554 at Chesterfield.

As a player, although short in stature, he was powerfully built and like many smaller batsmen was particularly strong playing the cut or pull shot. His best season with the bat came in 1896 when he scored 1,873 first-class runs (average 35.33). A first rate fielder at cover or point, he also bowled 'innocent' leg-breaks well enough to bring him 190 first-class wickets and a hat-trick. His weakness was temperament. His Australian success, suggested county captain Lord Hawke, 'turned his head' and, he added, 'perhaps he had more than an eye to his figures than the rest of us, though very keen to play the game.'

Personally, Brown was a quiet, pleasant-mannered man who still possessed the sense of humour characteristic of Yorkshire cricketers then. Certainly popular, 40,000 people attended his benefit match in 1901, from which he received £2,282, a county record at the time. A heavy-smoking asthmatic, he became teetotal almost overnight, emptying his remaining beer down the kitchen sink. He was forced to drop out of cricket in May 1904 due to heart trouble which, at first, was not considered serious but he never fully recovered and died in November of that year, aged thirty-five, from 'congestion of the brain and heart failure'. Jack Brown did have a prodigious and sometimes single-minded appetite for runs, which brought him 17,582 first-class runs including 29 first-class centuries, but as *Wisden* commented 'he was, whether he scored fast or slowly, an excellent bat to look at.'

Ronnie Burnet

RHB and OB, 1958-1959

Full Name: John Ronald Burnet, OBE
Birth: Saltaire, Bradford, 11/10/1918
Death: Greenhow Hill, Pateley Bridge, 07/03/1999

Type of Player: Lower middle order right-hand batsman, right-arm off-break bowler

First Class Career for Yorkshire:
Debut: v. MCC, Lord's, 1958
Matches: 54
Batting: 889 runs (Av. 12.88) Highest Score: 54 v. Hampshire, Bournemouth, 1958
Bowling: 1 wkt (Av. 26.00). Best performance: 1-8 v. Lancashire, Bramall Lane, Sheffield, 1959
Fielding: 7 catches
Year of last match: 1959

Tests: Nil

Appointed county captain in 1958 at the age of thirty-nine, without having appeared previously in first-class cricket, Burnet was charged with restoring spirit and harmony within the Yorkshire dressing room and he more than fulfilled his set objective. A hard-hitting batsman, Burnet moved to Baildon in the early 1930s and graduated to the club captaincy in 1949, leading them to a hat-trick of Bradford League titles as the 1950s unfolded, together with a Priestley Cup triumph in 1952.

His reputation as a leader brought him the Yorkshire Second XI captaincy in 1953 and through his enthusiasm, plus some talented Colts, he led them to the Minor Counties Championship in 1957. By the time of his appointment to the Yorkshire captaincy, Burnet's batting had deteriorated and he was slow in the field. Yet Brian Sellers and the committee felt he possessed the necessary qualities to re-establish the 'team' focus that had been lacking under Billy Sutcliffe's leadership. He came with a reputation as a strong taskmaster who put the interests of team and club before that of individuals. That stance quickly brought conflict and by the end of a difficult first season, when Yorkshire finished outside the top ten of the Championship for only the second time in their history, Wardle (senior pro and Burnet's main dissenter) had been sacked and both Appleyard and Lowson had played their last matches for the county. Close, Illingworth, Vic Wilson, Trueman and Binks formed the experienced nucleus still at Burnet's disposal as the 1959 season began, now combined with the best of the youthful young talent that had emerged under his leadership of the Second XI. A thrilling, successful chase for 215 in only 105 minutes against Sussex in the last match of the summer brought Yorkshire their first Championship title for thirteen years.

Burnet averaged only 11.47 with the bat in 1959; he took only six catches and captured one wicket in two overs, but his influence instilled a belief in the Yorkshire side that, by playing positive cricket, the Championship could be won. Thereafter he stepped down, joining the Yorkshire committee in 1960. Serving until 1969, he found his second spell less enjoyable. During the conflict that plagued the club in the 1980s, Burnet's endeavours, as part of Yorkshire's cricket committee, to resolve the discord arising from the Boycott crisis, failed. Awarded the OBE for his services as chairman of the Yorkshire and Humberside Sports Council, Burnet is rightly credited with laying the foundations for the emergence of a Yorkshire team that dominated the 1960s.

David Byas

LHB and RM, 1986-present

Full Name: David Byas
Birth: Kilham, Driffield, 26/08/1963

Type of Player: Middle order left-hand batsman, right-arm medium pace bowler

First Class Career for Yorkshire:
Debut: v. Glamorgan, Headingley, 1986
Matches: 252
Batting: 13,545 runs (Av. 34.91), 24 centuries. Highest Score: 213 v. Worcestershire, Scarborough, 1995
Bowling: 12 wkts (Av. 59.91). Best performance: 3-55 v. Derbyshire, Chesterfield, 1990
Fielding: 313 catches

Tests: Nil

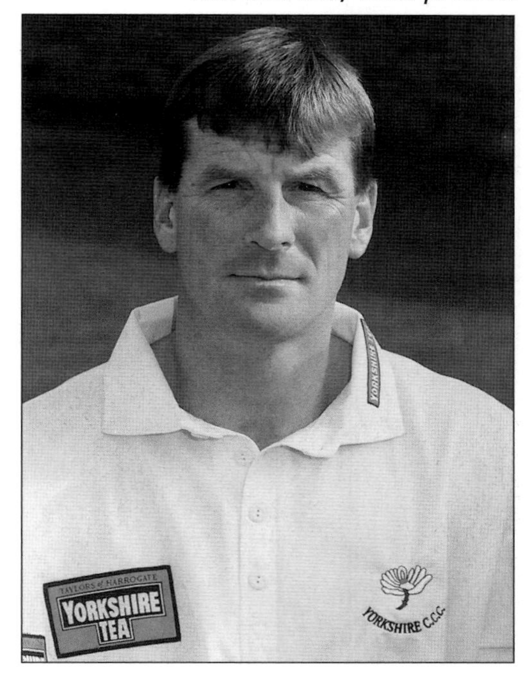

One of the toughest competitors of recent years, David Byas succeeded to the Yorkshire captaincy in 1996. Although the trophy cabinet remains bare under his leadership, his success can be measured by the way he has welded an excellent team spirit and ensured the development of several youngsters into good county professionals, and, in some cases, players of international pedigree. Byas attended Scarborough College and played for the club of the same town, being appointed captain in 1987 at the age of twenty-three – clearly young, but with obvious potential. He had made his county debut during the previous season but a duck in his only innings meant that he did not get another chance until 1988. He struggled for three seasons and made the breakthrough in 1991 with over 1,500 runs and the presentation of his county cap.

His attacking strokes are played with great power and he uses his height (6 ft 4 in) to get his body over the ball or play it strongly 'over the top' into the outfield. He has been particularly effective in this manner in limited-overs cricket, when he has often opened the batting. Although he was disturbed by clever spinners in his early days, he worked hard to overcome his technical difficulties and became regarded as one of the best left-handers on the county circuit, coming close to Test selection in 1995 – his best season, with 1,913 runs (average 56.26). Bravery has always been one of his qualities and he has never flinched from bowling of the highest pace and meanest hostility. Another string to Byas' bow is his fine slip fielding: in terms of catches per match only Sharpe and Tunnicliffe lie ahead of him. He has a very safe pair of hands and his agility belies his height. His 112 catches in limited-overs matches are a record for the county. His 7,185 (average 30.19) runs in these games have only been bettered by Boycott and Moxon.

He led Yorkshire to third in the County Championship in 1998 and 2000 (their best positions since 1975) and second in the National League in 2000. Frustratingly, he has captained the team in four losing semi-finals and one losing final in his five years in charge. For a leader with the highest percentage of wins for Yorkshire, in both forms of the game, since 1962, this is doubly frustrating. Should Byas receive a trophy, it would be extremely well-deserved for this strong but modest and popular man.

Phil Carrick

RHB and SLA, 1970-1993

Full Name: Philip Carrick
Birth: Armley, Leeds, 16/07/1952
Death: Steeton, Keighley, 11/01/2000

Type of Player: Lower-middle order right-hand batsman, slow left-arm bowler

First Class Career for Yorkshire:
Debut: v. Gloucestershire, County Ground, Bristol, 1970
Matches: 425
Batting: 9,994 runs (Av. 22.66), 3 centuries. Highest Score: 131* v. Northamptonshire., Northampton, 1980
Bowling: 1018 wkts (Av. 29.99), 5wi 42 times. Best performance: 8-33 v. Cambridge University, Fenner's, 1973
Fielding: 183 catches
Year of last match: 1993

Tests: Nil

In the last three decades of the twentieth century Yorkshire won only two major trophies. One of these was held aloft by a quiet, unassuming man – Phil Carrick. He led the county for three seasons and his great day came in the first of these, 1987, when the county won a nail-biting Benson & Hedges Cup final against Northamptonshire by the narrowest possible margin – with the fewest wickets lost in a tied match. After studying at Park Lane College, and playing for Farsley, he made an early breakthrough into the Yorkshire side and his best season came as early as 1975. He was an important factor in the county gaining runners-up spot in the Championship, his 79 wickets (average 21.17) being the highest aggregate. In fact, he and his spin-twin, Cope, took 47 per cent of Yorkshire's wickets during that campaign. He was awarded his cap during the following winter, while he was in South Africa!

Carrick's early style was very much in the tradition of giving the ball air and making every attempt to deceive the batsman by flight as well as turn. As his career developed, however, which was coincidental with the increased covering of wickets, he was increasingly expected to operate in a defensive mode, aiming at, or around, leg-stump. One of the consequences of this was that he became a very economical limited-overs bowler, but its negativity was a frustrating aspect. Entitled to be referred to as an all-rounder, his dogged batting brought him success, often when others had failed. It was to his frustration that he ended up just six runs short of the 10,000- and 1,000-wicket double for the county, although he did achieve it in all first-class cricket. Over 2,000 runs and 200 wickets in limited-overs matches meant that he was one of only two Yorkshire players to achieve that particular landmark.

Carrick's 1985 benefit brought him £73,020. He was appreciated as a thoughtful and undemonstrative cricketer and it was these qualities which were to the fore in his captaincy. The team made immediate progress under his leadership as their 1987 Championship position – eighth – was their best for seven years. He also spent valuable time urging the committee to sign an overseas player and always had the interests of the club at heart. He was on the first-class umpires reserve list at the time of his death, still being devoted to the game he served loyally.

Brian Close

LHB and RM/OB, 1949-1970

Full Name: Dennis Brian Close, CBE
Birth: Rawdon, Leeds, 24/02/1931

Type of Player: Opening/middle order left-hand batsman, right-arm medium pace/off-break bowler

First Class Career for Yorkshire:
Debut: v. Cambridge University, Fenner's, 1949
Matches: 536
Batting: 22,650 runs (Av. 31.94), 33 centuries.
Highest Score: 198 v. Surrey, The Oval 1960
Bowling: 967 wkts (Av. 24.29), 5wi 40 times.
Best performance: 8-41 v. Kent, Headingley, 1959
Fielding: 564 catches
Year of last match: 1970

Tests: 22, 1949-1976

There have been few cricketers more determined, tough and courageous than the likeable Brian Close. A naturally talented all-round cricketer – powerful batsman, brave and fearless close fielder and medium pace or off-spin bowler – he was a shrewd and strong captain who led the county to four Championship crowns and two Gillette Cup triumphs between 1963 and 1969. By the age of eleven, Close was playing in the Rawdon side, before he went on to develop his cricket and soccer talent at Aireborough Grammar School. He played both games for England schools and was signed as a professional footballer with Leeds United and then Arsenal before playing a few times for Bradford City. A knee injury effectively ended his soccer career.

He made his county cricket debut alongside Trueman and Lowson at Fenner's in May 1949. It was to prove an eventful maiden season. At the age of eighteen, Close did the 'double' for Yorkshire, scoring 1,098 runs and taking 113 wickets. He remains the youngest to achieve this feat and the only player to do so in his first season. Selected for the Third Test against New Zealand at Manchester that summer, he became – and remains – the youngest player to represent England. Blessed with an inborn talent for cricket, he completed his second 'double' for Yorkshire in 1952. However, his early potential perhaps remained unfulfilled as an all-rounder and he never again recorded a 1,000 runs and a 100 wickets in a season after that. As a batsman alone, however, he scored in excess of 1,000 runs in a season 13 times for Yorkshire. His best return came in 1961 with 1,985 first-class runs at an average of 35.44. That was also his benefit year, which brought in £8,154.

Two years later Close was appointed Yorkshire captain. One attribute he brought to his captaincy was flair. He was willing to try anything, whether that was changing the bowling or moving a fielder for no apparent reason – anything that might bring a result and very often did. The Championship title came in Close's first season in charge; Yorkshire winning 13 of the 28 matches in their centenary year, and for Close recognition as a *Wisden* Cricketer of the Year in 1964 who commented 'Almost overnight it seemed that Brian Close matured. He showed a knowledge of his own team and the play of opponents which immediately stamped him as a thinker and tactician.' After his youthful Test debut his appearances for England were sporadic. An ill-

Brian Close was a fearless and brave fielder, particularly in any position close to the wicket. Here he is shown (with his foot on the pitch) at silly mid-off for Yorkshire against Derbyshire in 1964.

judged shot against Benaud at Old Trafford in 1961 contributed to an unexpected defeat against Australia but it seemed against the West Indies in 1963 that he had finally established himself. His unflinching innings of 70, his highest Test score, at Lord's against the West Indian quicks Wes Hall and Charlie Griffith left him covered in bruises but won him national respect after one of the most memorable draws in Test cricket history. Asked to captain England in the last Test, again against the West Indies, at The Oval in 1966 he did an exceptional job. England won by an innings and he retained the role against India and Pakistan the following summer. Five of the six Tests were won by England. Close lost the England captaincy as a disciplinary measure after using delaying tactics in a Championship match against Warwickshire and despite a record of six wins and a draw he was replaced by Colin Cowdrey for the winter tour of the Caribbean.

The last three of his 22 Test caps came some nine years later when he was recalled at the age of forty-five to once more face a rampant West Indian pace attack, now led by Andy Roberts and Michael Holding. His final Test knock lasted 162 merciless minutes as he chested away several quick short deliveries but England were crushed by 425 runs and once more Close was amongst the scapegoats. If bravery was evident in Close's battles against the West Indies, his fielding close to the wicket sometimes boarded on the suicidal! His fearlessness at a very close short square leg has spawned several stories of catches taken at slip off Close's forehead. In that department, amongst others, he undoubtedly led by example.

Close's successful reign as Yorkshire skipper came to an abrupt and controversial end in 1970 when the committee announced that he would not be reappointed for the following season. He left to play at Somerset, where he led the county until his eventual retirement in 1977 when he was also awarded the CBE for Services to Cricket. One of the players who developed under his leadership at Somerset was a certain I.T. Botham who paid tribute to his mentor in his own autobiography, 'In fact, I would go so far as to say that starting out with Closey was vital for me because he taught me so much about attitude. He was the toughest man I ever played sport with or against.' His full first-class record brought him 34,994 runs (average 33.26) and 1,171 wickets at just over 26 apiece.

His final first-class appearance came in 1986 at the age of fifty-five at Scarborough, to bring to an end a career which spanned 37 years 115 days in total. After a brief spell as a Test selector (1979-81) he returned to serve Yorkshire once more, this time as chairman of the cricket committee in the 1980s and 1990s.

Geoff Cope

RHB and OB, 1966-1980

Full Name: Geoffrey Alan Cope
Birth: Burmantofts, Leeds, 23/02/1947

Type of Player: Lower order right-hand batsman, right-arm off-break bowler

First Class Career for Yorkshire:
Debut: v. Hampshire, Bradford, 1966
Matches: 230
Batting: 2,241 runs (Av. 14.00). Highest Score: 77 v. Essex, Middlesbrough, 1977
Bowling: 630 wkts (Av. 24.80), 5wi 33 times. Best performance: 8-73 v. Gloucestershire, County Ground, Bristol, 1975
Fielding: 64 catches
Year of last match: 1980

Tests: 3, 1977/78

First-class cricketers experience peaks and troughs during their careers. Off-spinner Geoff Cope endured more than most and, through his philosophical and phlegmatic approach, emerged as one of the most admirable characters in the game during the 1970s. As a youth, Cope was good at soccer and cricket but, having gambled on a career in the latter, he sacrificed a secure job with a Leeds firm of paper manufacturers and made his debut for Yorkshire in 1966. He headed the county averages a year later with 40 wickets (average 13.82) and by 1968 seemed the logical successor to Ray Illingworth who, having failed to secure a long term contract with Yorkshire, departed for Leicestershire.

Cope was first reported for alleged 'throwing' in 1968. A loss of form and confidence followed, but having been capped he enjoyed a resurgence in 1970 with 83 first-class wickets at 25.43 apiece, including a hat-trick against Essex at Colchester. He was twice suspended by the TCCB for a suspect bowling action – firstly in 1972 and again in 1978. Both times he fought hard to save his career and, with the help of his 'boyhood idol' Johnny Wardle, he remodelled his action. Cope's friendship with Wardle blossomed into a father-and-son relationship. With the Yorkshire veteran's support – he said: 'If we do this right, Geoff, you'll play for England' – and his own determination he returned to county cricket in 1973. Brighter days were ahead.

His career best innings bowling figures came at Bristol in 1975 when he took 8 for 73 against Gloucestershire. The hot summer of 1976 saw him end the season as the country's leading wicket-taker (93 wickets) and he was selected for England's winter tour of India. A Test berth did not come his way and he flew home when his father died. His Test chance finally came the following winter on England's tour to Pakistan and New Zealand when he came close to a hat-trick on his debut at Lahore. Having dismissed Abdul Qadir and Sarfraz Nawaz with successive balls, he had Iqbal Qasim given out, caught at slip off his next delivery – only for the fielder, captain Mike Brearley, to withdraw the appeal. His three Test caps all came during that series against Pakistan. His stubborn tail-end batting often saw him performing the nightwatchman's role and he passed 50 in first-class cricket five times. A joint benefit season with Barrie Leadbeater in 1980 yielded £33,846, in his final summer of first-class cricket. Thereafter he played Minor Counties cricket for Lincolnshire and today can be heard commentating on Yorkshire cricket for BBC Radio Leeds. He is also a member of the Yorkshire CCC committee.

Alex Coxon

RHB and RMF, 1945-1950

Full Name: Alexander Coxon
Birth: Huddersfield, 18/01/1916

Type of Player: Lower order right-hand batsman, right-arm medium fast bowler

First Class Career for Yorkshire:
Debut: v. Lancashire, Bradford, 1945
Matches: 142
Batting: 2,747 runs (Av. 18.43) Highest Score: 83 v. Nottinghamshire, Headingley, 1948
Bowling: 464 wkts (Av. 20.53), 5wi 24 times. Best performance: 8-31 v. Worcestershire, Headingley, 1946
Fielding: 124 catches
Year of last match: 1950

Tests: 1, 1948

A temperamental fast-medium right-arm bowler, Alec Coxon grabbed his chance to play for Yorkshire when it came after the Second World War and gave his all for the county over the next five seasons to 1950.

Coxon was born in Huddersfield and educated at Moldgreen School. He joined Yorkshire having had various spells in league cricket at Dalton, Meltham, Brighouse and Saltaire. His best innings analysis came at Headingley in 1946 when, as *Wisden* observed, he bowled 'with fair speed, length and spin' in taking 8 for 31 against Worcestershire. He ended the visitors' second innings with a hat-trick. Coxon's tireless, hostile and whole-hearted bowling brought this praise from Yorkshire cricket writer J.M. Kilburn at the end of that 1946 season: 'he lacked nothing in endeavour whatever may have been his shortcomings in artistry. For the most part his success came from persistence.'

His county cap was awarded in 1947 and presented in an unconventional way. As he reached the crease in Yorkshire's second innings against Sussex at Bradford in mid-May, captain Brian Sellers beckoned him down the pitch, took off his cap and offered it to Coxon with the words 'Try that for a fit'. Despite the honour, Coxon was dismissed for nought to complete a 'pair' although his bowling had brought him six wickets in the match. His 80 wickets that season cost just over 23 apiece.

Twice he took 100 wickets in a season for Yorkshire – 101 in 1949 and his best return, 129, a year later. Although his bowling perhaps lacked the pace needed to sustain him at the highest level, he did win one Test cap against Bradman's Australians at Lord's. His three Test wickets (Sidney Barnes, Arthur Morris and W.A. Brown) cost him 172 runs in the match and for years after there was a rumour of a clash with Denis Compton in the dressing room during that game. A well-equipped late-order batsman who averaged just over 18 in first-class cricket, the highest of his 13 half centuries came for Yorkshire against Nottinghamshire in 1948 when he made 83 out of his side's first innings 177 all out total.

He was thirty-four years of age when he left Yorkshire in 1950, and he played for Durham county between 1951 and 1954. He also played for Sunderland and between 1952 and 1954 took over 100 wickets in each season for the club.

David Denton

RHB and RMF, 1894-1920

Full Name: David Denton
Birth: Thornes, Wakefield, 04/07/1874
Death: Thornes, Wakefield, 16/02/1950

Type of Player: Middle order right-hand batsman, right-arm medium fast bowler

First Class Career for Yorkshire:
Debut: v. Warwickshire, Bramall Lane, Sheffield, 1894
Matches: 676
Batting: 33,282 runs (Av. 33.38), 61 centuries. Highest Score: 221 v. Kent, Tunbridge Wells, 1912
Bowling: 34 wkts (Av. 28.14), 5wi once. Best performance: 5-42 v. South of England, Scarborough, 1896
Fielding: 360 catches, 1 stumping
Year of last match: 1920

Tests: 11, 1905-1909/10

D. DENTON (Yorks.)

Described at times as a 'lucky' batsman, David Denton's record in first-class cricket and for Yorkshire conflicts sharply with that description. Only Herbert Sutcliffe, amongst Yorkshire batsmen, scored more runs for the county than Denton. Denton played his early cricket with the soapmakers Hodgson & Simpson at his home club, Thornes, near Wakefield. His elder brother, Joe, played two seasons for the county with only moderate success in the late 1880s and his younger brother became the second Denton to represent Yorkshire when he made his county debut.

Originally recommended as a bowler, Denton the batsman secured a regular county place in 1895 and there he stayed for another quarter of a century. A vital member of nine Championship-winning Yorkshire sides, he notched up 69 first-class centuries (61 for his county) and passed 1,000 runs in a season 21 times during his long career. His best season was 1905 (2,405 runs at 42.19 per innings) which was rewarded with selection amongst *Wisden*'s 1906 Five Cricketers of the Year. Three times in his career he scored a century in each innings of a match and the highest of his three first-class double centuries, which were all for Yorkshire, was made in 1912. He may possibly have surpassed that score at Worcester in June 1920. When Yorkshire's declaration came at 472 for 3, he was left on 209 not out but later remarked: 'What good purpose could be served by beating my own record?' Denton himself considered his best knock the 96 made for Yorkshire at Bramall Lane against Roses rivals Lancashire in 1905. Having surrendered a first innings lead of 101, the home side, thanks to Denton and Rhodes (74), emerged victors by 44 runs. Two years later came a benefit, raising £1,915, and in 1914 he shared a county record fourth-wicket partnership of 312 with George Hirst against Hampshire at Southampton.

Denton's batting was nothing if not adventurous. A slightly-built cricketer, he was a stylish, bold middle-order batsman who gave the opposition a chance and enjoyed his fair share of luck, but used that to prosper. *Wisden* in its 1906 tribute described him thus: 'Denton is essentially a brilliant player, possessing rare hitting power and a great variety of strokes. He scores indeed with equal facility all round the wicket. Thanks to

David Denton at the crease – only Herbert Sutcliffe has scored more first-class runs for Yorkshire.

his strong flexible wrists he makes the most of every opening on the off-side when the ground is hard and on slow wickets he can pull and play the hook stroke with the utmost effect. With him there is no waste of time, his big scores being nearly always made at a quick rate.' In the field he was exceptional in the deep and rarely dropped a catch. Very quick on his feet, his speed and accuracy of return placed him amongst the best of his era. The Yorkshire cricket writer A.W. Pullin ('Old Ebor') was moved to comment: 'If Denton dropped a catch the cricket world wondered.' Denton himself considered the best catch he took was at Taunton when he ran fifteen yards to catch one-handed Somerset's Lionel Palairet 'with one hand touching my boot-toe'.

As a Test cricketer, Denton was capped 11 times for England and was probably denied more Test caps by his Lancashire contemporary Johnny Tyldesley. Lord Hawke, Denton's county captain, compared the two in his *Recollections and Reminiscences*: 'There was always a lot of rivalry suggested between the skill of Johnny Tyldesley and David Denton, in which the latter never took the slightest interest. On a good wicket there was little to choose, and less in fielding. But on a mud pitch Johnny Tyldesley was wonderful; for instance, his century at Birmingham in the Test Match of 1905, whilst David under similar conditions would not have been feeling too comfortable. At all times Johnny might seem a trifle the sounder. Both were the most attractive professional batsmen of my time.' Only once did Denton feature in a home Test match for his country when he made 0 and 12 against Australia at Leeds. He toured South Africa in 1905/06 and again in 1909/10 when he made his only Test century at Johannesburg. His 104 took just 100 minutes and was in fact his third hundred in successive first-class innings.

But for ill health he would have continued playing for Yorkshire after 1920, having reached forty-six years of age. But he did not stray far from the game he loved. Unable to take up a coaching position due to poor health, he became Yorkshire's scorer for a time and then a first-class umpire from 1925 until 1937. A keen Methodist, he retained much of the cricket memorabilia that came his way during his career and his home in Denby Dale Road, Wakefield was filled with mementoes and photographs from his playing days.

Reckoned to be a shrewd man, he left more than £10,000 when he died in 1950. Those critics who perceived that Yorkshire batsmen of Denton's time were dull were left in no such doubt when he walked to the crease and played one of those dashing innings that brought him over 33,000 runs for his county, lucky or otherwise.

Arthur Dolphin

RHB and WK, 1905-1927

Full Name: Arthur Dolphin
Birth: Wilsden, Bradford, 24/12/1885
Death: Lilycroft, Heaton, Bradford, 23/10/1942

Type of Player: Lower order right-hand batsman, wicketkeeper

First Class Career for Yorkshire:
Debut: v. Cambridge University, Fenner's, 1905
Matches: 427
Batting: 3,325 runs (Av. 11.50) Highest Score: 66 v. Essex, Leyton, 1914
Bowling: 1 wkt (Av. 28.00). Best performance: 1-18 v. Sussex, Hove, 1910
Wicket-keeping: 569 catches, 260 stumpings
Year of last match: 1927

Tests: 1, 1920/21

The worthy successor to David Hunter as Yorkshire's wicketkeeper, Arthur Dolphin gave loyal service to the county for twenty-two years. His ability behind the stumps was considered almost equal to that of contemporary, Herbert Strudwick (Surrey). In his long career he was an integral part of eight Championship-winning Yorkshire sides. The first Bradford League player to represent Yorkshire, Dolphin was fourteen when he first played for Wilsden Britannia and nineteen when he made his county debut. He took over from Hunter as Yorkshire's first choice 'keeper in 1910.

A short, lively cricketer, few wicketkeepers of his time had to deal with the variety of bowling that confronted Dolphin. Amongst the left-handed bowlers he kept to were Hirst, Rhodes, Waddington, Drake and Kilner and with them came differing challenges of pace, swerve, spin and swing. In addition to that were Schofield Haigh and Macaulay with their medium paced off-breaks. With a minimum of fuss and effort he dealt with them all.

Herbert Sutcliffe observed Dolphin's true skill and wrote: 'His quick brain and exceptionally keen eyesight were responsible for disposing of large numbers of batsmen from chances which many 'keepers would have missed without even affecting their reputations.' His speed standing up to the wicket is underlined by the high proportion of stumpings he made for Yorkshire – 31 per cent. Another example illustrating his talent came against Hampshire at Leeds in 1921. When Hampshire made 456 for 2 in a day, Dolphin retained his concentration throughout and conceded just 2 byes in the innings.

He served alongside his county colleagues, Roy Kilner and Major Booth, with the 'Leeds Pals' in the First World War, but returned to Yorkshire in 1919. He enjoyed his most successful season with the gloves, claiming 82 dismissals in the first post-war summer. An obstinate lower order batsman, two of his best performances came against Essex at Leyton. In 1914, batting as the nightwatchman, he added 124 for the second wicket with B.B. Wilson and in 1919 contributed 62 not out in a last-wicket stand of 103 – with E. Smith – which averted the follow-on. His only Test cap came at Melbourne against Australia in the Fourth Test of England's catastrophic 1920/21 tour, although in retirement he stood in six Tests as an umpire. His benefit season in 1922 brought him £1,891. At various times during his career he suffered from sciatica and he played his last match for Yorkshire in 1927. During his decade as a popular first-class umpire he was renowned for never wearing a hat even on the hottest day.

Alonzo Drake

LHB and SLA, 1909-1914

Full Name: Alonzo Drake
Birth: Parkgate, Rotherham, 16/04/1884
Death: Honley, Huddersfield, 14/02/1919

Type of Player: Middle order left-hand batsman, left-arm slow medium bowler

First Class Career for Yorkshire:
Debut: v. Derbyshire, Bramall Lane, Sheffield, 1909
Matches: 156
Batting: 4789 runs (Av. 21.76), 3 centuries.
Highest Score: 147* v. Derbyshire, Chesterfield, 1911
Bowling: 479 wkts (Av. 18.00), 5wi 29 times.
Best performance: 10-35 v. Somerset, Weston-super-Mare, 1914
Fielding: 93 catches
Year of last match: 1914

Tests: Nil

The career of Alonzo Drake was meteoric and at times dazzling. At his best, in the right conditions, his bowling was devastating but at other times, when wickets or runs didn't come his way, despondency showed in his play. A talented soccer player in his youth, Drake had spells with a number of football clubs including Sheffield United, Birmingham City and QPR.

His sporting ability extended equally to cricket. He played with Aldwarke Park near his Rotherham home and later with Sheffield United before marriage took him to Honley, near Huddersfield. His club performances at Honley Cricket Club brought selection for the Yorkshire Second team in 1908 and the club identified sufficient talent to assign him to Harrogate CC for the 1909 season. His first appearance for Yorkshire in August that year was an auspicious entrance to county cricket. He scored 54 and took 4 for 34 in Derbyshire's first innings, standing in for George Hirst who was being rested. His progress was relatively sedate in 1910, but he announced his batting proficiency in 1911 with two first-class centuries, 115 against Sussex and his career best 147 not out at Chesterfield.

A powerful hitter with a strong off-drive, his 1,487 runs that summer included eight scores of 50 or more in addition to his two centuries. As a bowler he seemed to have reached his zenith in 1913 when he captured 100 wickets in a season for the first time and once more passed the 1,000 run mark. Amongst his best bowling efforts were 8 for 59 at Bristol against Gloucestershire and 7 for 69 against Essex at Bradford. On a helpful pitch Drake was deadly. He had a natural swing in his delivery and could make the ball break both ways. On good pitches, though, he was generally less effective. He eclipsed all that had gone before in what would prove his final summer playing first-class cricket for Yorkshire. In amongst his 158 wickets (at 15.30) was a remarkable bowling performance at Weston-super-Mare, where he returned match figures of 15 for 51, and in Somerset's second innings he became the first Yorkshire bowler to capture all ten wickets in an innings.

A heavy smoker, he was twice rejected by the army following the outbreak of war in 1914. His health continued to decline and before cricket commenced again in 1919 he was in his grave. A complex character, Drake was a natural all-round cricketer. At times a somewhat fatalistic and melancholy figure, he nevertheless left his mark on Yorkshire's record book in his relatively brief career.

Tom Emmett

LHB and LF, 1866-1888

Full Name: Thomas Emmett*
Birth: Halifax, 03/09/1841
Death: Leicester, 30/06/1904

Type of Player: Middle order left-hand batsman, left-arm fast bowler

First Class Career for Yorkshire:
Debut: v. Nottinghamshire, Trent Bridge, 1866
Matches: 298
Batting: 6,315 runs (Av. 15.10), 1 century.
Highest Score: 104 v. Gloucestershire, Clifton College, 1873
Bowling: 1,208 wkts (Av. 12.78), 5wi 92 times.
Best performance: 9-23 v. Cambridgeshire,Hunslet, 1869
Fielding: 177 catches
Year of last match: 1888

Tests: 7, 1876/77-1881/82

That T. Emmett be 'made captain in the absence of a Gentleman' read one of the minutes from a Yorkshire committee meeting in the close season of 1877/78. Although this statement appears ambiguous, the result was that Emmett led the side for five years and was the last professional captain of the county until 1960. Emmett was a very enthusiastic player; Haygarth, in *Scores and Biographies*, stated that he 'hits hard, bowls hard, runs hard and works hard'. He worked up pace in the early part of his career which involved spells with Illingworth, Halifax, Keighley and Todmorden clubs. Making his first-class debut at the late age of twenty-four meant that he was able to make an immediate impact, not only with 5 for 33 in his first game but also by heading the county bowling averages for each of his first two seasons.

Selection for one of the unofficial England teams followed in 1867 and the establishment of his partnership with Freeman resulted in one of the most feared opening attacks ever seen in county cricket. In 1868 Emmett and Freeman ran through the might of Lancashire, dismissing them for 30 and 34; Emmett bowled unchanged throughout a match on six occasions with Freeman and five times with Hill, a later partner. Emmett's bowling repertoire was full of variety; he would change the angle of attack by using the width of the crease and sometimes bowled from behind the line to deceive the batsman by length. He was also probably one of the first bowlers to bowl wide of the off-stump in order to obtain an edge and his degree of experimentation was such that waywardness was often a consequence. The motto, ' First a wide and then a wicket', became attributed to him. His best ball pitched on middle-and-leg and hit the off-stump and was much admired by W.G. Grace, who feared it even when well-set.

Style and flair were both very much features of Emmett's make-up. He was very popular with the crowds and was regarded as the best-loved player of his time, after Grace. His quips became part of folklore and when the latter scored 318 against the county, Emmett's response was, 'Grace before meat, Grace after meat and Grace all b***** day'. Yorkshire were not a particularly efficient side in the field and, on one generous day, Emmett could only comment, 'There's an epidemic here and it ain't catching'. Emmett's attacking batting also contributed to his value to the side, especially when it was felt his technique was good enough

The Yorkshire team in 1885. From left to right, back row: G. Ulyett, R. Peel, W.H. Woodhouse, H. Turner (scorer), J. Hunter. Middle row: W. Bates, E. Peate, L. Hall (captain), T. Emmett, F. Lee. Front row: J.M. Preston, T. Grimshaw. Tom Emmett himself captained Yorkshire from 1878 to 1882.

to open the innings for a time.

His entire Test career was played in Australia, including the very first such game of all. His best performance at this level – 7 for 68 at Melbourne – was on his second tour. Even into his late thirties and forties, the success rate in Emmett's bowling did not diminish. Despite his lessening of pace he was able to impart even greater movement. His powers of leadership were not so commanding, however. Although he was able to lift the team with his cheerful approach, his lack of firmness told on occasions. The team was a collection of talented individuals but did not always play as a unit, being just as capable of humiliating defeats as notable victories. Nine counties tended to be included in various versions of the Championship and Yorkshire's best efforts under Emmett were third place in each of his two final seasons, according to the late Roy Webber.

The ending of his tenure was a little muddled when it became obvious that the Hon. M.B. Hawke would be taking over the reins. The latter played under Emmett for the 1882 season but Hawke took over during the following campaign on coming down from Cambridge and the roles were thus swapped. The two men, with their very different backgrounds, formed a relationship based on mutual respect rather than close friendship but it could never completely be Hawke's side while Emmett remained in the team. By the mid-1880s Emmett's powers were fading, and after retiring he was able to remain in the game by coaching at Rugby School and Leicestershire. In the former institution one of his pupils was a certain Pelham Warner, who recalled him to be 'a character ... with ... merry eyes [and] an attractive laugh.' He felt that Emmett allowed the boys to develop naturally and without rigidity.

Emmett was the first bowler to take 1,000 wickets for Yorkshire and no one to complete the feat since has done so at a better average. His final tally in all first-class matches was 1,572 (average 13.57). The figures are impressive but more so was the way he played the game. The last word rests with Hawke, who said of Emmett: '...the greatest character that ever stepped on a cricket field, a merry wag who could never lose heart nor temper'.

George Freeman

RHB and RF, 1865-1880

Full Name: George Freeman
Birth: Boroughbridge, 28/07/1843
Death: Sowerby Grange, Thirsk, 18/11/1895

Type of Player: Middle order right-hand batsman, right-arm fast bowler

First Class Career for Yorkshire:
Debut: v. Cambridgeshire, Ashton-under-Lyne, 1865
Matches: 32
Batting: 752 runs (Av. 14.46). Highest Score: 53 v. Nottinghamshire, Trent Bridge, 1868
Bowling: 209+4 wkts (Av. 9.94), 5wi 24 times. Best performance: 8-11 v. Lancashire, Holbeck, 1868
Fielding: 16 catches
Year of last match: 1880

Tests: Nil

Despite a short career, George Freeman is regarded as one of Yorkshire's greatest fast bowlers. W.G. Grace was in no doubt and stated that he was 'the finest bowler I have ever played against ... his bowling came quickly off the pitch and the spin he got on it troubled me more than any other bowler.'

In his youth Freeman had such natural talent that his easy action, coming off a few paces, brought him many wickets for his home town club. In 1863 he took a post at Grange House School, Edinburgh, but he was not suited to Scotland. His career break came when he played in a match at York on a home visit; he made such an impression that employment was found for him locally and he obtained a Yorkshire trial.

By the time he entered the county game, Freeman had matured into a player with a powerful physique. He stood at almost six foot and weighed over fourteen stones. He had the ability to keep the ball low and was extremely accurate, the batsmen often being hit if their wickets were not struck.

His best season came as early as 1867 when he took 51 wickets (average 7.45) in only six matches. It was a remarkable average, even taking into account the poor pitches of the time. In the following season his match figures of 12 for 23 were the main factors in Lancashire being dismissed for 30 and 34. Freeman's only tour was in the autumn of 1868, to North America, where 74 of his 104 victims were bowled. As an aggressive batsman, his most telling performance came against Surrey in 1869; his 51 was made in a total of 82 and his match figures of 13-60 led his side to victory.

After the 1871 season Freeman decided to devote his energy to his business. He continued to make occasional appearances and in his final game for Yorkshire, a non-first-class match in 1881, an innings of 60 and 9 wickets showed that none of his old powers had waned.

In a mere five full seasons Freeman had made a tremendous impact. His mark, literally and figuratively, was made on the game and many batsmen suffered as a consequence. One of them, a certain C.E. Green, of the MCC, was reputed to have carried a bruise for the remaining forty-seven years of his life after an innings against the best fast bowler of his time.

Paul Gibb

RHB and WK, 1935-1946

Full Name: Paul Antony Gibb
Birth: Acomb, York, 11/07/1913
Death: Guildford, Surrey, 07/12/1977

Type of Player: Opening/middle order right-hand batsman, wicketkeeper

First Class Career for Yorkshire:
Debut: v. Nottinghamshire, Bramall Lane, Sheffield, 1935
Matches: 36
Batting: 1,545 runs (Av. 32.87), 2 centuries. Highest Score: 157* v. Nottinghamshire, Bramall Lane, Sheffield, 1935
Bowling: 3 wkts (Av. 27.33). Best performance: 2-40 v. Jamaica, Melbourne Park, Kingston, 1935/36
Wicketkeeping: 25 catches, 8 stumpings
Year of last match: 1946

Tests: 8, 1938/39-1946/47

One of the least-known of Yorkshire's England opening batsmen, and wicketkeepers, Paul Gibb holds some unique records and would undoubtedly have played more but for the Second World War. Gibb's home was in Brandsby, North Yorkshire, but he attended St Edward's School, Oxford. He made his first-class debut for Scotland against the Australians in 1934 and went up to Cambridge as a contemporary of Yardley. Gibb gained a blue in his first summer and also made his debut for Yorkshire, scoring what was to be his highest innings for the county and becoming the only amateur to make a century in his first match for Yorkshire.

Despite such promise, Gibb's university commitments, Yorkshire's strength and the war meant that he never even gained a county cap. However, because of his amateur status and the unavailability of Sellers and Yardley, he had the honour of being captain on Yorkshire's first-ever overseas tour, to Jamaica in 1935/36. Gibb's batting helped him gain the wicketkeeping place for the 1936 Varsity match, as well as for the Gentlemen later on. 1938 was his best first-class season – 1,658 runs, including his highest score, 204 for the University against the Free Foresters – and during it he was chosen to replace the injured Les Ames as England 'keeper. Although the match was abandoned, Gibb gained a place on the tour to South Africa the following winter. He made his Test debut at Johannesburg and scored 93 and 106, becoming the first Yorkshire player to score a century in his first Test. He played in all five Tests and also made a century in the last – the 'Timeless Test' at Durban.

After the war Gibb played one more season for Yorkshire, latterly as senior 'keeper, and was then lost to the game. He re-appeared in 1951, but as a professional for Essex. After five seasons he became an umpire and also coached in South Africa, one of his pupils being Mike Procter. He concluded his career with 12,520 runs and 548 dismissals and many of Gibb's contemporaries held him in high regard. Hutton praised his defensive technique and stated that when well-set he could score all round the wicket. He was brave as a 'keeper, being quick to get into position and very good standing up to the wicket. He was devoted to the game, to which 'few have given more thought or effort'.

Darren Gough

RHB and RFM, 1989-present

Full Name: Darren Gough
Birth: Barnsley, 18/09/1970

Type of Player: Lower order right-hand batsman, right-arm fast medium bowler

First Class Career for Yorkshire:
Debut: v. Middlesex, Lord's, 1989
Matches: 114
Batting: 2,247 runs (Av. 18.12), 1 century. Highest Score: 121 v. Warwickshire, Headingley, 1996
Bowling: 378 wkts (Av. 26.65), 5wi 14 times. Best performance: 7-28 v. Lancashire, Headingley, 1995
Fielding: 24 catches

Tests: 49, 1994-2000/01

A charismatic, spirited and likeable quick bowler from Barnsley, Darren Gough once described himself honestly as 'an entertainer' and few followers of Yorkshire and English cricket would argue otherwise. At Priory Comprehensive school in Monk Bretton, Gough was a talented sports player, excellent at football, rugby and athletics as well as cricket. His ability at football saw him trial at Rotherham Town as a midfielder. When that didn't work out, an opportunity to move into cricket came his way at Headingley on a YTS scheme and subsequently as a member of the Yorkshire Cricket Academy.

'Dazzler', as he was nicknamed, made his county debut aged eighteen. The raw teenager made an encouraging start, taking five wickets in the match, including Mike Gatting amongst his victims. A stress fracture quickly curtailed his season, however, and his progress and development was slow thereafter (81 first-class wickets at 39 apiece) until a career-changing transformation begun in 1993. He lost a stone in weight and became both fitter and quicker. His line and length improved; suddenly the two bad balls per over disappeared from his game and, encouraged to bowl quickly by Yorkshire's West Indian overseas player Richie Richardson, he finished the summer with 57 wickets at 26.61 apiece. He was capped by Yorkshire, selected for England's 'A' tour of South Africa that winter and married in October – a big year all round. By the end of the South African tour he was a first choice player and, having made his one-day debut for England against New Zealand in May 1994, won his first Test cap in the Third Test at Old Trafford against the same opponents. His batting brought early plaudits with 65 in his first Test innings and he took a wicket in his first over.

The Australians took a liking to the lively Yorkshireman on England's Ashes tour of 1994/95, particularly after his whirlwind 51 and 6 for 49 at Sydney. 'Gough's gumption has caught the imagination in Australia. They are used to their Poms being diffident and diplomatic, not brash and brimming with bravado like their own sportsmen' wrote the *Daily Express*. An injured left foot brought a premature end to Gough's tour and an attempt to make a rapid comeback in 1995 ended again with injury. Not called upon by England for the Tests

Darren Gough, pictured in the Yorkshire Phoenix National League strip, returns to his bowling mark.

against India and Pakistan in 1996, Gough claimed 66 Championship wickets at an average of 22.69 and recorded his first county hundred (121 including 4 sixes and 11 fours) against Warwickshire at Leeds. Against South Africa in 1998 he stormed back to his best at international level and in the series decider at Headingley tore in to finish with 6 for 42 in the South Africans' second innings. That analysis included his five hundredth first-class wicket and his one hundredth Test victim, Jonty Rhodes. He played an important part again in England's victory over Australia at Melbourne in late 1998 and started the new year with a hat-trick in the Test at Sydney, the first for England against Australia since 1899.

Chairman of selectors David Graveney referred to the broad-shouldered paceman as 'the pulse of the team'. Gough, at 5 ft 11 in, tends to skid the ball through but is consistently the quickest of England's bowlers. He has mastered the off-cutter but uses it sparingly and effectively as he does the late reverse inswinging yorker, often best employed in the closing stages of a limited-overs match. A prankster at times, Gough transmits his obvious enjoyment of playing the game, a rare commodity in modern sport. As Matthew Engel wrote in *Wisden* 1999, having chosen him as one of the almanack's Five Cricketers of the Year: 'Above all, though, in a team of brooders and worriers, he stood out for his bullish enthusiasm.'

By the end of England's winter tours, Gough had 138 one day international wickets and 197 Test scalps to his credit, making him an essential part of the national side. With the advent of the ECB central contracts, Yorkshire's loss (only three Championship appearances in 2000) was England's gain. Fully fit all season he formed, with Andrew Caddick, a formidable opening attack that helped secure a Test rubber win over the West Indies for the first time since 1969. Gough, with 25 wickets at just over 21 apiece, was chosen as England's Man of the Series. On the dusty, generally unresponsive wickets of the sub-continent (Pakistan and Sri Lanka, 2000/01) Gough still played a major role. Ten wickets in the series victory in Pakistan was eclipsed by a tally of 14 wickets at 19.57 each in Sri Lanka, an achievement which brought him another 'Man of the Series' award.

Above all else Darren Gough remains an uncomplicated and wholehearted cricketer, willing to give his all for county and country whenever and wherever he is called upon to serve. Yorkshire CCC has awarded him a well-deserved benefit in 2001, which coincides with the publication of his autobiography.

Andrew Greenwood

RHB, 1869-1880

Full Name: Andrew Greenwood*
Birth: Cowmes Lepton, Huddersfield, 20/08/1847
Death: Huddersfield, 12/02/1889

Type of Player: Opening/middle order right-hand batsman

First Class Career for Yorkshire:
Debut: v. Nottinghamshire, Trent Bridge, 1869
Matches: 94
Batting: 2,755 runs (Av. 18.00). Highest Score: 91 v. Gloucestershire, Bramall Lane, Sheffield, 1877
Bowling: 0 wkts
Fielding: 33 catches
Year of last match: 1880

Tests: 2, 1876/77

Five Yorkshiremen played in the first-ever Test match and Andrew Greenwood, on his second tour of Australia, was one of two in that team who came from the Lascelles Hall Club. Greenwood opened the batting in the second innings and was successful in the Second Test with scores of 49 and 22 in a four-wicket win.

Greenwood took some time to establish himself in the Yorkshire side but his brilliant out-fielding was to his advantage. In 1871 an innings of 50 in the Roses match confirmed his promise and he gained selection for a North XI in a match against XV Colts of England with Luke Greenwood (his uncle), and carried his bat for 40 not out in a score of 78.

The following season brought further honour when he played in the prestigious North against South match at Canterbury. Again, it was his fielding which took the eye, being 'really brilliant and saved the North many runs'. Greenwood's batting contribution was a score of 52 made out of 79 while he was at the wicket. In the meantime had come another significant innings for the county – a score of 56 against the MCC. The season after his first trip to Australia brought Greenwood his highest aggregate – 456 runs. His highest scores were all in county games, the best being 78 not out against Lancashire at Bradford. He had by now developed a sound technique, was a regular in the side and often performed well in adversity.

In 1876, however, Greenwood's form for Yorkshire fell away and this decline for the county meant that he never really fulfilled his potential for them; but he made the only first-class century of his career – in a North against South game – with a score of 111. Following Greenwood's Test experience he achieved his best season's average as he topped the Yorkshire batting with 373 runs at 26.90. His highest first-class score for the county came when he opened the batting and was last out in an 'example of wonderfully patient defence'. By this time he was regarded as 'one of the best professional batsmen in England ... a thorough cricketer' according to *Lillywhite's Annual*. Greenwood did not live for many more years after his final game but he was able to reflect on his valuable contributions on the difficult wickets of the time in the most demanding position – the top of the order.

Schofield Haigh

RHB and RFM/OB, 1895-1913

Full Name: Schofield Haigh
Birth: Berry Brow, Huddersfield, 19/03/1871
Death: Taylor Hill, Huddersfield, 27/02/1921

Type of Player: Lower-middle order right-hand batsman, right-arm fast medium/off-break bowler

First Class Career for Yorkshire:
Debut: v. Derbyshire, Derby, 1895
Matches: 513
Batting: 10,993 runs (Av. 19.05), 4 centuries.
Highest Score: 159 v. Nottinghamshire, Bramall Lane, Sheffield, 1901
Bowling: 1,876 wkts (Av. 15.61), 5wi 127 times.
Best performance: 9-25 v. Gloucestershire, Headingley, 1912
Fielding: 276 catches
Year of last match: 1913

Tests: 11, 1898/99-1912

Dubbed the 'sunshine of the Yorkshire XI', Schofield Haigh, alongside the mighty Kirkheaton pair Rhodes and Hirst, formed a formidable trio of bowlers that gave Lord Hawke's side of the Golden Age such dominance. A right-arm fast-medium pace bowler with the ability to bowl a sharp turning off-break, Haigh came from Berry Brow, Huddersfield.

Coached as a youngster by Louis Hall, the former Yorkshire opening batsman, Haigh developed his playing skills in Scotland with Aberdeen and Perth before his county debut. An underrated batsman, he made almost 11,000 runs for the county including four centuries. His off-drive was considered one of the finest in county cricket and he was able to defend stubbornly or attack when the occasion demanded. However, it was his bowling that really won him fame. At the start of his career he bowled quickly off a long run but later shortened his run and slowed his pace. His off-cutter on a sticky wicket made him almost unplayable, and was described by A.A. Thomson as being 'like the kick of a horse'. He also had in his armoury a devastating yorker, which he perhaps under used.

Haigh's first significant bowling effort came against the Australians at Bradford in 1896 when he took 8 for 78. The following summer he produced one of his best bowling performances in taking 7 for 17 against Surrey at Leeds, all his victims being bowled in 12 overs. Eleven times in his career he took 100 wickets in a season, with a best return of 174 wickets at 14.59 in 1906. Haigh's somewhat limited Test appearances (between 1899 and 1912) indicate that he never made his mark at that level – 113 runs and 24 wickets at 25.91 apiece. He toured South Africa twice and on the first trip picked up his Test best bowling figures (6 for 11) at Cape Town in April 1899. Selection as one of *Wisden*'s five – along with three other Yorkshiremen! – in 1901 and a well-deserved benefit in 1909, which provided £2,071, were other major landmarks in Haigh's career.

He was a popular coach at Winchester College until shortly before his unexpected death. Haigh's son, Reg, went on to become president of the Huddersfield League and served on the Yorkshire county committee. There was much more to this sportsman than statistical achievement. 'There was no nicer professional cricketer' said Plum Warner. A man of humour, he was a friendly, modest cricketer who seemed always to have a smile on his face whatever the state of the game.

Louis Hall

RHB and SRA, 1873-1894

Full Name: Louis Hall*
Birth: Batley, 01/11/1852
Death: Morecambe, Lancashire, 19/11/1915

Type of Player: Opening right-hand batsman, right-arm slow lob bowler

First Class Career for Yorkshire:
Debut: v. Middlesex, Prince's, London, 1873
Matches: 279
Batting: 9,999 runs (Av. 23.52), 10 centuries.
Highest Score: 160 v. Lancashire, Bradford, 1887
Bowling: 22 wkts (Av. 39.81). Best performance: 4-51 v. Liverpool and District, Aigburth, 1892
Fielding: 174 catches
Year of last match: 1894

Tests: Nil

One of the dourest batsmen ever, Louis Hall carried his bat through a completed innings on fifteen occasions, including fourteen for Yorkshire. This is a total which has been beaten by only two players in the history of first-class cricket. Hall made a few appearances in his debut season, but was then neglected for five years. In the meantime he acted as professional for Perth in Scotland.

The turning point came when he scored 79 in a club match against the Australians in 1878. Thereafter, he was a permanent fixture in the team and established the county's first regular opening partnership with Ulyett. They created a world record by being the first pair to make two century opening partnerships in the same match, against Sussex at Hove in 1885, and shared twelve such stands together. The pair played in contrasting styles, Hall being solid and slow. Innings of 12 in 165 minutes and 29 in 210 minutes bear this out, as does his playing fourteen consecutive maidens against George Davidson of Derbyshire. Although he was not outstandingly tall, his slim build made him appear a commanding figure.

His best season was 1887, when he scored 1,240 runs, at an average of 38.75. His bowling was only occasionally productive, but in the game containing his highest score, he followed this up with match figures of 7 for 147. In contrast, his fielding was brilliant, especially close to the wicket. Hall often captained Yorkshire shrewdly when Lord Hawke was absent and set a good example to the younger players, being a teetotaller and Methodist preacher. He helped retired players through being chairman of the Cricketers' Benevolent Fund. One of his acts of charity was in allowing his own benefit to be postponed so that Bates, after the damage to his eye, could receive priority. When Hall's turn came – he was the first to be granted a benefit by the Yorkshire CCC committee – in 1891, his reward was £570.

On retirement Hall became a coach at Uppingham School and also a first-class umpire for seven seasons. Although his batting had included some strong legside shots and he later felt that he could have used them more often, there is no doubting his value to the side. Five of his scores when he carried his bat were under 40 – clear evidence that when others failed on bowlers' pitches, he was often still there.

Harry Halliday

RHB and OB, 1938-1953

Full Name: Harry Halliday
Birth: Pudsey, 09/02/1920
Death: Stanley, Wakefield, 27/08/1967

Type of Player: Middle order right-hand batsman, right-arm off-break bowler

First Class Career for Yorkshire:
Debut: v. Glamorgan, Cardiff Arms Park, 1938
Matches: 182
Batting: 8,361 runs (Av. 32.03), 12 centuries. Highest Score: 144 v. Derbyshire, Chesterfield, 1950
Bowling: 101 wkts (Av. 30.88), 5wi twice. Best performance: 6-79 v. Derbyshire, Bramall Lane, Sheffield, 1952
Fielding: 140 catches
Year of last match: 1953

Tests: Nil

Like many cricketers who started their first-class careers in the late 1930s, Harry Halliday was robbed of perhaps his best days in county cricket by the Second World War. Born in Pudsey, Halliday was a stylish middle order right-hand batsman, off-break bowler and good slip fielder; another product of Pudsey St Lawrence CC. At the age of eighteen he scored 36 in his debut innings for Yorkshire against Glamorgan at Cardiff, in 1938. During the war, Halliday played with success for the British Empire XI, topping their batting averages in 1943 and 1944. *Wisden* 1945 reviewed Halliday's batting thus: 'Halliday, sound in method, hit the ball harder than in 1943 and seldom failed.' Against London Counties in July 1944 he scored a century at Lord's (101 not out), driving with tremendous power.

Halliday became a regular member of the Yorkshire first XI in 1947. The first of his 12 first-class centuries came in 1948. Opening the batting he scored 130 at Bristol against Gloucestershire. By the close of that season he had 1,357 runs and a further three hundreds to his name and was rewarded with his county cap. The summer of 1950 was Halliday's best, 1,484 runs at an average of 38.05. His one century that year was his career highest 144 at Chesterfield in Yorkshire's seven-wicket victory over Derbyshire. Off-driving firmly he batted for just over four hours.

A model of consistency in both 1952 and 1953, he scored five further hundreds for Yorkshire in those two seasons and also passed the 1,000 run mark in both. He developed his off-spinners to such a degree that in 1952 his tally of 41 wickets was the third highest return for Yorkshire after Close (98) and Wardle (158). His career best bowling was also recorded that season, 6 for 79 against Derbyshire at Bramall Lane, where he 'turned his off-breaks sharply' and scored 74 in a fine all-round display.

A testimonial came Halliday's way in 1954, earning £2,500, although his last appearance for Yorkshire was in 1953. When his county days were behind him he put his coaching experience (gained in South Africa) to good use and had professional engagements at Workington and Cumberland. He also coached at Scarborough College and Scarborough CC. A promising pre-war batsman, Halliday gave good service to Yorkshire, particularly between 1947 and 1953, although he perhaps never fulfilled his youthful promise.

Gavin Hamilton

LHB and RFM, 1994-present

Full Name: Gavin Mark Hamilton
Birth: Broxburn, Scotland, 16/09/1974

Type of Player: Lower middle order left-hand batsman, right-arm fast medium bowler

First Class Career for Yorkshire:
Debut: v. Kent, Maidstone, 1994
Matches: 62
Batting: 2023 runs (Av. 29.75), 1 century. Highest Score: 125 v. Hampshire, Headingley, 2000
Bowling: 195 wkts (Av. 24.32), 5wi 7 times. Best performance: 7-50 v. Surrey, Headingley, 1998
Fielding: 23 catches

Tests: 1, 1999/2000

The latter part of the 1998 season proved to be a turning point in Gavin Hamilton's career. He improved his career-best bowling performance three times in consecutive matches, taking five wickets in an innings four times. He also scored five half-centuries in the final eight games. The highlight of this outstanding form was against Glamorgan at Cardiff. Hamilton scored 79 and 70 and took 5 for 69 and 5 for 43. He was the first player to score two half-centuries and take ten wickets in the same match for Yorkshire since 1906.

Hamilton's route to Yorkshire had been somewhat circuitous. A birthplace north of the border was followed by schooling in Hurstmere, Kent and club cricket with Sidcup. A return to Scotland on leaving school led to the West Lothian club and his first-class debut, for Scotland, in 1993, when he took 5 for 65 against Ireland at Eglington. Jack van Geloven, a local umpire, recommended the promising youngster to Yorkshire and with Scotland's coach being Love, further reference was readily available. The county nurtured his potential carefully through the Academy and Second XI until the 1998 explosion. Scotland's qualification for the 1999 World Cup left Hamilton in a dilemma. They were keen for him to play and Hamilton wanted to but also wanted his future to be with England. A new ruling, allowing players to appear for associate-member countries without prejudicing their future with a Test-playing team saved the day. Hamilton had a brilliant World Cup with the bat; his 217 runs (average 54.25) included half-centuries against Bangladesh (63) and the might of Pakistan (76). His bowling was not so successful, however, with only three wickets in the five games.

Hamilton is an attacking player by instinct. His batting shows a full array of shots and his bowling, with movement both ways off the seam, is designed for taking wickets. Sadly these qualities remained unused when he played his only Test match, in South Africa. He suffered a pair and bowled unsuccessfully and expensively, despite being used in a partly defensive capacity. This opportunity had come after another successful season when he was the only player in the top fifteen of both the batting and bowling national first-class averages. He is just as effective in limited-overs cricket; for Yorkshire he has so far totalled 726 runs and 102 wickets, his best being 5 for 16 against Hampshire at Headingley in 1998. Hamilton could have expected to make his one-day international debut for England but became injured at a vital time. However, he is young and capable enough for his chance to come again.

John Hampshire

RHB and LB, 1961-1981

Full Name: John Harry Hampshire
Birth: Thurnscoe, South Yorkshire, 10/02/1941

Type of Player: Middle order right-hand batsman, right-arm leg-break bowler

First Class Career for Yorkshire:
Debut: v. Leicestershire, Grace Road, Leicester, 1961
Matches: 456
Batting: 21,979 runs (Av. 34.61), 34 centuries.
Highest Score: 183* v. Sussex, Hove, 1971
Bowling: 24 wkts (Av. 46.16), 5wi twice.
Best performance: 7-52 v. Glamorgan, Cardiff Arms Park, 1963
Fielding: 368 catches
Year of last match: 1981

Tests: 8, 1969-1975

A player who scores a century in his first Test ought not to be dropped after his second. That was the fate suffered by John Hampshire. An innings of 107 against the West Indies at Lord's was the prelude to appearances in five different series as this talented batsman suffered selectoral inconsistencies. Schooling at Oakwood Technical High and appearances for Rotherham Town preceded Hampshire's county career. He was used as an opener early on but it was soon felt that his attacking style was better suited to the middle order. His strong shoulders and forearms produced powerful pulling and hooking and he drove attractively on both sides of the wicket. Against this, however, was perceived an inability to concentrate and his first century did not come until 1965.

Hampshire enjoyed his cricket with the successful side of the 1960s but the following decade was in complete contrast. He suddenly found himself a senior player in a sour dressing-room atmosphere. Although 1978, with 1,596 runs at 53.20, was his best season, it was more notable for the infamous Northampton go-slow. Hampshire deliberately batted so slowly, in protest at Boycott's tactics, that Yorkshire missed a bonus point. Although the committee criticised Hampshire's actions, he was rewarded with the captaincy when Boycott was sacked at the end of the season. The subsequent two years were the least happy of Hampshire's career; although Yorkshire reached two semi-finals and respectable positions in the Championship, the pro-Boycott faction gave him a very unpleasant time. He certainly had a sound tactical approach but his leadership seemed to lack flair. His resignation was followed by a season in the ranks, before he spent three years with Derbyshire.

As a batsman he was very suited to limited-overs cricket and his seven centuries are a Yorkshire record. His 6,248 runs (average 31.88) place him fourth on the county list. His attacking nature made him popular with spectators and his 1976 benefit netted him £28,425. Although his wrist-spin was rarely used, he did contribute two match-winning spells. He was also an outstanding fielder, specialising at short leg. Hampshire joined the first-class umpires list on retirement and stood in his first Test four years later. He became so well-respected in this second career that he was promoted to the international panel in 2000. Despite his ups and downs in the game, this was just reward for a man still dedicated to cricket forty years after his debut.

Peter Hartley

RHB and RMF, 1985-1997

Full Name: Peter John Hartley
Birth: Keighley, 18/04/1960

Type of Player: Lower order right-hand batsman, right-arm medium fast bowler

First Class Career for Yorkshire:
Debut: v. Surrey, Abbeydale Park, Sheffield, 1985
Matches: 195
Batting: 3,844 runs (Av. 20.66), 2 centuries.
Highest Score: 127* v. Lancashire, Old Trafford, 1988
Bowling: 579 wkts (Av. 30.11), 5wi 21 times.
Best performance: 9-41 v. Derbyshire, Chesterfield, 1995
Fielding: 60 catches
Year of last match: 1997

Tests: Nil

One of the unsung heroes of the county circuit, Peter Hartley plied his seam bowling trade with maximum effort. One of the most down-to-earth characters who ever represented Yorkshire, Hartley could be relied upon to give his best whatever the conditions and match situation. Hartley's early club cricket was with Keighley and Undercliffe but, after his education at Greenhead Grammar School and Bradford College, followed by rejection from Yorkshire, he went to Warwickshire. Two wickets in three matches was his lot for 1982, so he was not re-engaged. A winter in Australia followed by a letter to Padgett changed his fortunes. His debut meant that he became the first to represent Yorkshire after having played for another county.

In many respects it is surprising that Hartley was able to bowl for so long; his run-up has an appearance of stiffness and his action does not flow smoothly either. Although he managed to stay fit for most of his career, he did miss the 1989 season because of a back injury. He was, however, a player who improved with age. His best season was 1995 when he took 81 wickets at 22.97, his best performance including the hat-trick in a spell of five wickets in nine balls. The pitch was a seamer's paradise and even the opposing captain, Kim Barnett, was delighted for such an honest professional. Hartley's popularity was exemplified when Byas spoke out against the non-renewal of his contract at the end of 1997. Hartley's response was to sign for Hampshire where he has continued in the same reliable vein to the extent that, at the age of thirty-nine, he was voted player of the season for 1999, retiring the following year. Hartley's reward as the proceeds from his 1996 benefit was £107,500, as he continued to bowl his heart out for his county.

A sum of 280 wickets in limited-overs matches is the third-best total for Yorkshire, demonstrating his adaptability. His batting could not be relied upon for regular contributions but he was able to rescue Yorkshire from 37-6 on the occasion of his highest score and guide them to the safety of 224. He could certainly play quality strokes and gave the ball a good thump. Cricket has its supporting cast; there is no better example in Yorkshire cricket of someone enjoying this role and giving their all to it more than Peter Hartley.

Lord Hawke

RHB and LM, 1881-1911

Full Name: Hon. Martin Bladen Hawke (succeeded as 7th Baron Hawke 1887, thereafter known as Lord Hawke)*
Birth: Willingham Rectory, Gainsbrough, Lincolnshire, 16/08/1860
Death: West End, Edinburgh, 10/10/1938

Type of Player: Middle order right-hand batsman, left-arm medium pace bowler

First Class Career for Yorkshire:
Debut: v. MCC, Scarborough, 1881
Matches: 513
Batting: 13,197 runs (Av. 20.20), 10 centuries.
Highest Score: 166 v. Warwickshire, Edgbaston, 1896
Bowling: 0 wkts
Fielding: 159 catches
Year of last match: 1911

Tests: 5, 1895/96-1898/99

Probably the most influential person in the history of Yorkshire cricket, Lord Hawke was not even born in the county. A descendant of Admiral Hawke, who was created first baron after his victory at Quiberon Bay, his love of cricket began at prep school in Slough and continued at Eton, where he won his colours in 1878. In the meantime his family had moved to Wighill Park, Tadcaster and he played in the holidays for the Yorkshire Gentlemen. He went up to Cambridge at the age of twenty-one, won blues for three years and captained the University in his final season, 1885, when they beat Oxford by seven wickets.

Hawke had succeeded to the county captaincy in 1883, before finishing university, although he did not lead the side much until 1886. He was to hold the office for a record twenty-eight seasons and Yorkshire won the championship eight times under his leadership, including a hat-trick of titles beginning in 1900. His influence over his players began off the field of play and he eventually came to be better-known for his non-cricketing reforms rather than his captaincy during play itself.

The Yorkshire team was an undisciplined side when Hawke took over and it was a slow process to improve matters, especially in fielding. It took ten years for him to lift his first title, this being the county's first since the Championship had been officially constituted, and peaks were reached in 1900 and 1908 – not a single match was lost throughout both campaigns.

Hawke treated his professionals in a kindly manner, instituting changes that were to have repercussions for the game as a whole. His men were placed on a performance-bonus system by which marks were awarded during the season for outstanding individual efforts. Each season ended with an informal gathering at Wighill Park during which money was handed out on a pro-rata basis for the acccumulation of these marks. He also introduced winter payments – a very popular move – and encouraged his men to invest their benefit money wisely. This shrewd combination of concern for his players' financial welfare, allied to a strong sense of discipline earned him the respect of all who played under him. Even the sacked Peel bore him no malice. Hawke instituted the Yorkshire badge of the white rose with its eleven petals and, after his last season as captain, in 1910, he

The Yorkshire team of 1903. From left to right, back row: W.A.I. Washington, D. Hunter, J. Tunnicliffe, L. Whitehead, W. Rhodes. Middle row: G.H. Hirst, F.S. Jackson, Lord Hawke (captain), T.L. Taylor, S. Haigh. Front row: J.T. Brown, D. Denton. Yorkshire won eight Championship titles under Lord Hawke's leadership, including a hat-trick of county crowns between 1900 and 1902.

became the county president, holding that office until his death.

At the game's highest level his batting talents were negligible, but he was more than able to hold his own on the county scene. He scored his first century for Yorkshire in 1886 and topped the averages in 1890. His best aggregate for a season was five years later when he scored 1,078 runs at 23.95, and his highest innings contributed to the record score of 887. He enjoyed batting, revelling in his hard-hitting style – especially his driving – although he could late-cut with ease too. This was typical of the amateurs of the day, and was helped by his being tall, bulky and strong, although he could defend when the situation required.

Hawke was one of the first people to recognise the importance of making the game global. He led his own tours to North America, India, South Africa and West Indies and was the first to take a party to Argentina, in 1912. He led England in four of his five Tests (all in South Africa) and was victorious on each occasion. In 1899 he became the first chairman of England's Test selectors, holding the post for five series until 1909 and again in 1933. Only four men have chaired the committee for a longer period and only three of these have a better success-rate than Hawke. He insisted that the captain not be part of the selection process and always believed in a balanced side. 1899 was the year of the first five-Test series and Hawke was influential in the fact that Headingley was one of the grounds added to the list of Test venues.

He was president of the MCC during the Lord's centenary year of 1914 and continued to hold the post during the war years. He was treasurer for six years from 1932; but despite the high offices that he held and his title, snobbery was never part of his make-up. He upheld the high ideals of sport and encouraged his men to play to them. His famous comment hoping that no professional would ever captain England sums up the man less than when he stated, 'I think that sometimes cricket is too serious, that by becoming so important as a pursuit it loses its flavour as a sport. The moral character of my men is of infinitely more importance than their form.'

Allen Hill

RHB and RMF, 1871-1882

Full Name: Allen Hill*
Birth: Newton, Kirkheaton, Huddersfield, 14/11/1843
Death: Leyland, Lancashire, 28/08/1910

Type of Player: Lower order right-hand batsman, right-arm medium fast bowler

First Class Career for Yorkshire:
Debut: v. MCC, Lord's, 1871
Matches: 139
Batting: 1,695 runs (Av. 8.60). Highest Score: 49 v. Middlesex, Bramall Lane, Sheffield, 1876
Bowling: 537 wkts (Av. 12.96), 5wi 39 times. Best performance: 7-14 v. Surrey, Argyle St., Hull, 1879
Fielding: 91 catches
Year of last match: 1882

Tests: 2, 1876/77

Although Allen Hill shared the same birthplace as Hirst and Rhodes, he was another product of Lascelles Hall. His bowling developed quickly and he was playing professionally, at the age of seventeen, for Dewsbury, and then Mirfield, before taking up a post as coach and groundsman at Stonyhurst College. His next move was to join the Lancashire ground staff and he was a professional at Burnley when he made his Championship debut for Yorkshire.

Deputising for the injured Freeman, Hill's start could hardly have been more sensational. Figures of 6 for 33 and 6 for 24 (all 12 being bowled) plus a top score of 28 in Yorkshire's first innings of 100 were the major contribution in Surrey's home defeat by ten wickets. Evidence of this being no freak occurrence was provided by such performances as 6 for 9 against United South in 1874 and a spell of 5 for 3 in four overs against Lancashire in 1876. Freeman was not being missed as much as had been feared.

Despite a round-arm action and a short run-up, Hill had a model delivery; he bowled the occasional in-swinger but relied mostly on accuracy and pace. His final tally of victims in first-class cricket was 749 and he took three hat-tricks, including one for the Players. 1873 was his best season, with 82 wickets at 12.10. There were nine occasions when he bowled throughout a match with the same partner, showing that, despite his pace, he was able to bowl in sustained and penetrative spells.

Hill's best first-class bowling figures were in the important North against South game of 1874 at Prince's, when he took 8 for 48. In that same season he first turned out for the Players and his representative cricket peaked when he appeared in what became known as the first Test match. Although his final figures were undistinguished, he had the honour of taking the first wicket and the first catch – a record which can never be removed. He fared better in the second game when an innings analysis of 4 for 27 and a score of 49 helped England to victory.

Hill's benefit game in 1884 against Lancashire, where he had returned as a coach, raised £376, two years after his career had unfortunately ended as a result of a broken collar bone – a sad end for a very fine bowler.

George Hirst

RHB and LMF, 1891-1929

Full Name: George Herbert Hirst*
Birth: Kirkheaton, Huddersfield, 07/09/1871
Death: Lindley, Huddersfield, 10/05/1954

Type of Player: Middle order right-hand batsman, left-arm medium fast bowler

First Class Career for Yorkshire:
Debut: v. Somerset, Taunton, 1891
Matches: 718
Batting: 32,057 runs (Av. 34.73), 56 centuries.
Highest Score: 341 v. Leicestershire, Aylestone Road, Leicester, 1905
Bowling: 2,484 wkts (Av. 18.03), 5wi 174 times.
Best performance: 9-23 v. Lancashire, Headingley, 1910
Fielding: 520 catches
Year of last match: 1929

Tests: 24, 1897/98-1909

Only one player in the history of county cricket has ever scored more than 2,000 runs and taken 200 wickets in the same season – that player was George Herbert Hirst – one of cricket's greatest all-rounders. Like his county colleague Rhodes, George Herbert, as he was affectionately known, hailed from Kirkheaton, batted right-handed and bowled left-handed. His career record ensured immortality; Lord Hawke described Hirst as the 'greatest county cricketer of our time'. No fewer than nineteen times he scored over 1,000 runs in a season, going on to 2,000 on three occasions and in fifteen seasons he topped 100 wickets. He performed the 'double' 14 times – only Rhodes exceeded that tally.

Hirst left school at the age of ten and was in the Kirkheaton First XI by 1885. Professional engagements followed at Elland, Mirfield and Huddersfield. A short (5 ft 6 in.) but strongly built figure, he began his illustrious first-class career as a quick left-arm over bowler who batted late in the order for Yorkshire. It was his bowling which made the first real impact in 1893: 99 first-class wickets saw him finish behind only Peel and Wainwright in the county bowling averages. Against MCC at Lord's his match return was 12 for 48 and he took an innings best at Scarborough of 7 for 38, also against the MCC. His bowling initially progressed more rapidly than his batting although his first hundred for Yorkshire came in 1894, an unbeaten 115 at Bristol against W.G. Grace and Gloucestershire's best. The first of two career hat-tricks came the following season at Leicester amongst 150 first-class wickets that year.

Another landmark was conquered in 1896 with his first 'double' and he made his Test debut against Australia at Sydney in December 1897. By the dawn of the new century, Hirst was a fundamental part of Lord Hawke's powerful Yorkshire side. As a bowler, Hirst perfected a slower ball together with a viciously accurate yorker and by 1901 had mastered the art of swerve bowling and moved the ball prodigiously, particularly when new. His many helpless victims described it like 'a fast throw from cover point', so much was the movement. An aggressive but sure-footed batsman with a two-eyed stance, he said: 'I have been told I was a terrible offender against the orthodoxy of batting.' His strengths were certainly the hook and the pull. Yorkshire's highest individual score, 341 made in 1905 against Leicestershire, remains next to Hirst's name in the record books. His skill with bat

George Hirst, like his great county colleague Wilfred Rhodes, batted right-handed, bowled left-handed and hailed from Kirkheaton near Huddersfield.

and ball was matched with his ability in the field – 604 catches in all first-class matches – where he was outstanding at mid-off.

A loyal, tenacious and good humoured cricketer, Hirst was worshipped by his fellow Yorkshiremen and hugely respected by opponents. His benefit in 1904 harvested £3,703, a county record until 1925, and Lancashire switched the date of the game to the August Bank Holiday to ensure Hirst had the most lucrative fixture possible. Had he not been recognised amongst *Wisden*'s Five in 1901, his selection would have been a mere formality in 1906 when he reached the summit of his many achievements in county cricket. The unique feat of 2,385 runs and 208 wickets remains, and probably always will, the only time a player has performed the 'double double'. Asked if he thought any other cricketer would ever emulate his deeds that season, Hirst replied: 'I don't know, but whoever does will be very tired.'

Hirst's Test record was somewhat modest, it could be argued, for one so prolific at county level. His 59 wickets cost 30 each and his 790 runs were at an ordinary average of 22.57. Certainly on his two tours of Australia his swerve bowling was less effective than in England. In 1902 he and Rhodes bowled Australia out for 36 at Edgbaston and one of the most popular, but disclaimed, legends of Hirst's Test career came in the Oval Test of that series when he joined his county team-mate Wilfred Rhodes at the crease. Fifteen runs were still needed for victory and unofficial history claimed that Hirst instructed his partner 'We'll get 'em in singles'. Get them they did, though not all in singles.

Hirst's Test best with the bat was his 85 at Adelaide on the 1897/98 tour and 5 for 48 with the ball at Melbourne on the 1903/04 trip. Although Hirst's final first-class appearance was in 1929, after 1921 he began an eighteen-year engagement at Eton College, where his kindness and patience as a coach won him the everlasting admiration of many cricketers who improved as a result of his advice and support. Genial, warm, friendly and easily spoken, Hirst's broad dialect and humour were as memorable as his performances – his smile 'used to almost meet at the back of his neck.' A master of the game with bat and ball, his outstanding record was a mighty legacy.

Matthew Hoggard

RHB and RFM, 1996-present

Full Name: Matthew James Hoggard
Birth: Leeds, 31/12/1976

Type of Player: Tail-end right-hand batsman, right-arm fast medium bowler

First Class Career for Yorkshire:
Debut: v. South Africa 'A', Headingley, 1996
Matches: 34
Batting: 191 runs (Av. 6.16). Highest Score: 21 v. Somerset, Taunton, 1999
Bowling: 122 wkts (Av. 24.46), 5wi 4 times. Best performance: 5-47 v. Derbyshire, Derby, 1999.
Fielding: 8 catches

Tests: 1, 2000

Without so much as having gained a Yorkshire cap, Matthew Hoggard was thrust, in June 2000, into the limelight of the 100th Test match to be played at historic Lord's. Lasting only three days, the game ebbed and flowed, finally moving England's way as Hoggard sat with his pads on during a nail-biting but match-winning eighth-wicket stand of 31. Although he ended the match, against the West Indies, wicketless, he impressed with the movement he gained during his opening spell as well as his bravery during his first innings knock.

Hoggard's early cricket was learnt with Pudsey Congs, and he played a little at Grangefield School, Pudsey, but entered the Yorkshire Academy at the age of sixteen, gaining a Second XI contract in his second year. As an Under-19 he toured Zimbabwe, as a replacement, in 1995/96, and in the following summer played in two 'Tests' against New Zealand, taking 5 for 85 at Worcester, his victims including three future Test players.

Hoggard first came to attention in the professional game with a spell of bowling which brought him his first five-wicket haul in a Championship encounter – against Essex at Scarborough in 1998. In a pulsating match he was able to obtain extra bounce and movement, both of which troubled all the batsmen. More significantly, he was noticed by South Africans Hansie Cronje and Allan Donald as a net bowler for the Headingley Test and spent the following two winters as Free State's overseas player, learning from Donald in particular as well as contributing to on-field success.

1999 was a summer of frustration for Hoggard, being side-lined with injury for much of the campaign, but he bounced back in 2000 with a vengeance, gaining his county cap twenty days after his England one and enjoying his best season thus far, taking 50 first-class wickets at 26.46. He swung the ball in helpful conditions and contributed significantly in limited overs matches, taking a record 37 wickets (average 12.37) in the National League. Hoggard initially made his mark as Gough's reserve, but even with five England seam bowlers in Yorkshire's squad, he is no longer outshone by anyone. He has a strong body, a smooth and balanced run-up, and should prove one of the county's leading pacemen for several years to come.

Twenty wickets on the 2000/01 full England tour to Pakistan and Sri Lanka, at the outstanding average of 9.25, also show that he remains very close to the Test team.

Percy Holmes

RHB and RM, 1913-1933

Full Name: Percy Holmes
Birth: Oakes, Huddersfield, 25/11/1886
Death: Marsh, Huddersfield, 03/09/1971

Type of Player: Opening right-hand batsman, right-arm medium pace bowler

First Class Career for Yorkshire:
Debut: v. Middlesex, Lord's, 1913
Matches: 485
Batting: 26,220 runs (Av. 41.95), 60 centuries. Highest Score: 315* v. Middlesex, Lord's, 1925
Bowling: 1 wkt (Av. 124.00). Best performance: 1-5 v. Leicestershire, Aylestone Road, Leicester, 1922
Fielding: 319 catches
Year of last match: 1933

Tests: 7, 1921-1932

The senior half of Yorkshire's best opening pair of batsmen, Percy Holmes enjoyed being a contemporary of Herbert Sutcliffe but this, and competition from Surrey's Jack Hobbs and Andrew Sandham, meant that his international appearances were limited. Holmes' early cricket was with Paddock and Golcar and he first made an impact at senior level in 1919 when he and Sutcliffe created a new record stand for Roses matches, of 253 and selection as two of the 1920 *Wisden* Five Batsmen of the Year. They soon developed a virtually telepathic understanding when running together. With complete trust in each other, and neither having a recognised technical weakness nor dislike for any type of bowling, the pair could score at a brisk rate.

In 1920 Holmes became the first Yorkshire player to score two centuries in a match against Lancashire, and five years later his best season's aggregate of 2,453 included his career-best score which broke the 105-year-old record for the highest innings at the game's headquarters. Holmes' best Test series was in South Africa in 1927/28 when he opened with Sutcliffe in all five Tests. The highest score of his career (88) contributed to their only Test century stand together. Holmes returned home to his benefit season, which produced £2,620, and his best average of 58.42. The year 1932 brought Holmes and Sutcliffe the world record partnership for any wicket – against Essex at Leyton. After almost seven-and-a-half hours the pair passed Brown and Tunnicliffe, Sutcliffe played a tired shot and was bowled with the score on 555. Shortly afterwards the scoreboard slipped back to 554, but a lost no-ball was found and the new record was theirs, Holmes' contribution being 224.

Despite this, Holmes was to play for only one more season. Following an operation he was not fully fit and a top score of only 65 was made in the pair's final century stand together – their 74th in first-class cricket, which included 69 for Yorkshire and 64 in the Championship. Holmes then had a period in the Welsh League, a season as an umpire and coached at Scarborough College until the age of seventy. Even without Sutcliffe, Holmes' career was outstanding. He scored five of Yorkshire's highest ten innings and always batted with flair. His footwork was brilliant and he constantly looked to attack. His speed in the outfield concludes the image of one Yorkshire's most enthusiastic players.

David Hunter

RHB and WK, 1888-1909

Full Name: David Hunter*
Birth: Scarborough, 23/02/1860
Death: Northstead, Scarborough, 11/01/1927

Type of Player: Lower order right-hand batsman, wicketkeeper

First Class Career for Yorkshire:
Debut: v. MCC, Scarborough, 1888
Matches: 521
Batting: 4,239 runs (Av. 11.74). Highest Score: 58* v. Worcestershire, Worcester, 1900
Nottinghamshire
Bowling: 0 wkts
Wicketkeeping: 870 catches, 330 stumpings
Year of last match: 1909

Tests: Nil

Regarded as the best wicketkeeper never to play for England, David Hunter shone for Yorkshire over a lengthy period, during which the county began to exercise its pre-eminence over all other teams. Hunter's contribution was not just behind the stumps – vital in a successful side – but also in his capacity as occasional captain. He led the 1908 side in 17 of its 28 matches when the Championship was won without a single defeat. For several years he lived near the Scarborough ground and, like his brother, played for the town's club side before making his county debut.

Haigh, Hirst and Rhodes were the best contemporary trio of bowlers ever to play for Yorkshire. They were versatile and, to many batsmen, unreadable, yet Hunter coped brilliantly, even standing up to the wicket for at least the first half of his career. The batsman knew that he would not be allowed any room for error and the high percentage of stumpings in Hunter's dismissals shows his alertness. On four occasions he stumped five men in a match and against Surrey at Bradford in 1898 captured six victims by this method.

Despite being tall for a 'keeper, at just over six foot, he was alert and agile and his timing was such that there were no bruises on his hands, although he did not wear reinforcement tips inside his gloves. His powers of concentration were exemplary. Dick Lilley was the England 'keeper for most of Hunter's career and it was felt that the superiority of the former's batting kept winning the day. C.B. Fry confirmed what most felt, namely that Hunter was 'second to none in catching and stumping'. His batting was certainly not negligible and often showed stubborness as his four tenth-wicket century stands demonstrate: the 148 runs which he put on with Hawke against Kent at Bramall Lane in 1898 was a county record which stood for eighty-four years.

Hunter's 1897 benefit brought him £1,975 and after his retirement he coached at Scarborough. J.M. Kilburn remembered him being courteous and charming to young players of all ability. He was never to know the label that is now sadly his – the only major Yorkshire wicketkeeper never to represent his country. None of his rivals ever dismissed six batsmen in an innings, yet Hunter achieved the feat twice. His quiet and undemonstrative character belied his ability to pounce on the batsman's error in an instant.

Joseph Hunter

RHB and WK, 1878-1888

Full Name: Joseph Hunter
Birth: Scarborough, 03/08/1855
Death: Rotherham, 04/01/1891

Type of Player: Tail end right-hand batsman, wicketkeeper

First Class Career for Yorkshire:
Debut: v. Lancashire, Old Trafford, 1878
Matches: 143
Batting: 1,183 runs (Av. 7.78). Highest Score: 60* v. Gloucestershire, Bradford, 1885
Bowling: n/a
Wicketkeeping: 207 catches, 102 stumpings
Year of last match: 1888

Tests: 5, 1884/85

The eldest of five brothers, three of whom were wicketkeepers, Joe Hunter followed George Pinder behind the stumps for Yorkshire and made the position his own from 1881 until 1887. A stone-mason by trade, Hunter learnt his cricket with Scarborough CC where he played during the 1870s. Back then he was a regular opening batsman but it was his prowess as a wicketkeeper that attracted Yorkshire's interest. He came into the First XI as a replacement for Pinder and, in all, played ten matches that season. It took him a further three years before he became the regular first choice county 'keeper.

Although he never ranked as highly as Lancashire's Richard Pilling or Nottinghamshire's Sherwin, at his best Hunter was sound in style and execution and rarely let his side down. *Cricket* magazine in 1892, in recalling Hunter's career, stated that 'at one time he had no superior behind the stumps.' Almost a third of his wicketkeeping dismissals for Yorkshire were stumpings. He established a county record against Gloucestershire in 1887 taking nine catches in the match, an achievement not bettered until David Bairstow's eleven catches in 1982 – interestingly at Scarborough, Hunter's old nursery!

A regular number ten or eleven in the batting order, his best achievement with the willow came at Bradford in 1885 when he scored 60 not out versus Gloucestershire. He was invited to tour Australia with the Lillywhite, Shaw and Shrewsbury party in the winter of 1884/85 but was originally offered less-favourable terms than some of the other more prominent professionals. On the advice of Lord Hawke he held out for better terms and, having secured them, played in all five Tests on the trip. He averaged 18 with the bat, made 3 stumpings and took 8 catches behind the wicket as England won the series 3-2.

The successful 1887 season proved to be Hunter's last full summer for Yorkshire. Ill-health brought a rapid decline in his skills and he was succeeded in 1888 by his brother David. After retiring from county cricket he played a few more games for his home club Scarborough. Once landlord of the Wellington Inn at Scarborough, he kept the Wheat Sheaf pub in Rotherham before his premature death at the age of thirty-five. In a relatively short career, Joe Hunter received the one honour denied his younger brother – a Test cap. He served Yorkshire well in his brief time at the top and remains the only Scarborough-born player ever to play Test cricket.

Len Hutton

RHB and LB, 1934-1955

Full Name: Sir Leonard Hutton
Birth: Fulneck, Pudsey, 23/06/1916
Death: Norbiton, Kingston-on-Thames, Surrey, 06/09/1990

Type of Player: Opening right-hand batsman, right-arm leg-break bowler

First Class Career for Yorkshire:
Debut: v. Cambridge University, Fenner's, 1934
Matches: 341
Batting: 24,807 runs (Av. 53.34), 85 centuries.
Highest Score: 280* v. Hampshire, Bramall Lane, Sheffield, 1939
Bowling: 154 wkts (Av. 27.40), 5wi 4 times.
Best performance: 6-76 v. Leicestershire, Aylestone Road, Leicester, 1937
Fielding: 278 catches
Year of last match: 1955

Tests: 79, 1937-1954/55

When as distinguished a coach as Hirst claimed that he could not teach a young teenager anything about batting and the same youngster was described by Herbert Sutcliffe as 'a marvel, the discovery of a generation', contemporaries must have been left amazed by these remarks. They were referring to Len Hutton: at the age of sixteen he was opening the batting for Pudsey St Lawrence and making his county Second XI debut. He began with a duck (a habit which continued in his first innings for both Yorkshire and England) but his First XI debut followed in 1934, and he was soon moved up the order to open with Sutcliffe. In Hutton's first Championship game, against Warwickshire at Edgbaston, he scored 50 in his only innings and later became the youngest Yorkshire player to score a century with 196 against Worcestershire.

The 1935 season was slightly clouded by a minor operation and some loss of form, but his prowess returned the following year and he was rewarded with his county cap. Hutton's Test debut came against New Zealand and the 1938 season, which began by him being chosen as one of the *Wisden* Five, was made memorable by his famous 364 at The Oval against Australia. Don Bradman's 334, made at Headingley in 1930, had been overtaken by Wally Hammond's 336 not out in New Zealand and now Hutton claimed the world record, holding it for almost twenty years. He batted for over thirteen hours to achieve this feat; his career reached an early peak, confirmed by 12 centuries in 1939, only to be sadly cut short by war.

Hutton's outstanding batting technique was founded on a supreme defence and the ability to play every shot in the book to perfection. His cover drive was regarded as one of the most graceful and beautiful shots ever seen in cricket. His technical ability was such that he would succeed on the most treacherous pitches when others fell. A score of 30 when England were all out for 52 at The Oval against Australia in 1948 confirmed this. An accident in a gymnasium during the war was of such a serious nature that Hutton returned to cricket with his right arm two inches shorter. A technical adjustment was necessary but so accurate was this that there appeared to be no waning of his powers.

He formed a successful Test opening partnership with Cyril Washbrook and in

Len Hutton walks out to bat at Scarborough.

1949 produced his best-ever season: 1,294 runs in June set a still unbeaten record for any month and a total of 3,429 runs (average 68.58) were made in fine style. However, he was also beginning to be very aware of how much his wicket meant to both Yorkshire and England. Neither the Championship nor the Ashes were being won and he was needed more and more to play the anchor role.

1952 was a major turning point in English cricket when Hutton, a professional player, was appointed to lead the national side. Despite being the best candidate from a cricketing viewpoint, the election did not please traditionalists. He began well enough, winning three out of four Tests against India but the real test came a year later with the visit of Australia. Four draws, including a nail-biting encounter at Lord's, resulted and the sides came to The Oval level. A team-list of stars were victorious by eight wickets and Australia's nineteen-year grip on the little urn was over.

The following winter's tour to the West Indies was bedevilled with controversy, something which Hutton found discomforting. He rested for part of the 1954 season, as amateur David Sheppard led England, but was restored to the captaincy for the trip to Australia. Despite beginning with an innings defeat, after which he dropped the stalwart Alec Bedser, his young fast bowlers Frank Tyson and Brian Statham played the leading role in the Ashes being retained by three Tests to one. By now Hutton's efforts had taken their toll; he withdrew from the Test side for the 1955 season, played about half a campaign and announced his retirement the following January. The summer's birthday honours rewarded him with a knighthood and most of the rest of his life was spent away from the limelight, although he did serve as a Test selector for two years in the 1970s. He died just a few months after being elected Yorkshire's president.

Hutton's final tally of first-class runs was 40,140 (average 55.51) with 129 centuries, including 6,971 in Tests (average 56.67). He broke the Yorkshire record for a benefit with £9,712 in 1950 and this stood for twenty-three years. In all conditions and against all types of bowlers, Hutton was without doubt the best batsman in the county's history. In an all-time England XI, he would open the batting. A great knight, Sir Leonard.

Richard Hutton

RHB and RFM, 1962-1974

Full Name: Richard Anthony Hutton
Birth: Pudsey, 06/09/1942

Type of Player: Middle order right-hand batsman, right-arm fast medium bowler

First Class Career for Yorkshire:
Debut: v. Lancashire, Old Trafford, 1962
Matches: 208
Batting: 4,986 runs (Av. 20.18), 4 centuries.
Highest Score: 189 v. Pakistanis, Bradford, 1971
Bowling: 468 wkts (Av. 21.91), 5wi 17 times.
Best performance: 7-39 v. Somerset, Headingley, 1969
Fielding: 160 catches
Year of last match: 1974

Tests: 5, 1971

Compelled to live in his father's shadow, Richard Hutton, the eldest son of Leonard, was very much his 'own man' who developed into a tall (6 ft, 4.5 in.), strong and aggressive right-handed all-rounder for both Yorkshire and England. Born, like his father, in Pudsey, he attended Woodhall School, near Wetherby, before going on to become an outstanding schoolboy talent at Repton School – recognised as a fine establishment for cricket as well as education. From there his development continued at Christ's College, Cambridge. He made his first-class cricket debut in 1962 for the University against Essex in a Cambridge side that also contained Tony Lewis and Mike Brearley. Yorkshire gave him a debut in the Roses match later that season.

Hutton was a steady bowler in all conditions who concentrated on bowling at the wickets. With his height he was capable of extracting awkward lift and bounce and was proficient in the art of seam and swing bowling. His best first-class bowling figures of 8 for 50 were returned for Cambridge, rather than Yorkshire, against Derbyshire in 1963. He was also a first-rate slip fielder and as a batsman stood upright at the crease demonstrating a stylish off-drive. He hit 1,000 runs in a season twice, his 1,122 runs in 1963 at an average of 27.36 remaining his best. His four centuries for Yorkshire were all scored in the 1970s. He won all his Test caps in 1971 with appearances against Pakistan and India. At The Oval, in the Third Test against India, he and Alan Knott shared a stand of 103 in 66 minutes for the seventh wicket. His innings of 81 in that match was both his highest Test score and the perfect response to one critic who had told his father that he was not good enough to play at that level! He toured Australia in 1971/72 as part of the Rest of the World team.

A cricketer with a sharp sense of humour and devilish wit, his retirement was hastened by the appointment of Geoffrey Boycott as Yorkshire captain in 1971. Hutton's dislike of the captain's approach and methods eventually brought a premature close to his days as a Yorkshire player. A career in banking and accountancy followed and he was editorial director of *The Cricketer* magazine between 1991 and 1998. But for personal conflict within the dressing room, Richard Hutton might well have gone onto greater achievements within the game and in a different era may have attained the highest white rose honour – the captaincy of Yorkshire.

Roger Iddison

RHB and RF, 1853-1876

Full Name: Roger Iddison
Birth: Bedale, 15/09/1834
Death: York, 19/03/1890

Type of Player: Middle order right-hand batsman, right-arm fast/lob bowler

First Class Career for Yorkshire:
Debut: XIV of Yorkshire v. United England XI, Hyde Park, Sheffield, 1853
Matches: 80
Batting: 2,096 runs (Av. 19.41), 1 century.
Highest Score: 112 v. Cambridgeshire, Hunslet, 1869
Bowling: 106+1 wkts (Av. 15.47), 5wi 4 times.
Best performance: 7-30 v. Nottinghamshire, Bradford, 1863
Fielding: 79 catches
Year of last match: 1876

Tests: Nil

Roger Iddison had the honour of being Yorkshire CCC's first captain. Although he only missed seven games in his ten-year tenure, the informality of the period meant that he could quite happily play for another county, even Lancashire, while still being official club captain!

Iddison's early development was such that he played for XIV of Yorkshire against the United All-England XI while aged only eighteen and later took part in the first-ever tour of Australia in 1861/62. He was very much a fast, round-arm bowler at this stage but later bowled slow lobs. He had a prodigious break produced by a ball that appeared to come from a pocket just below his arm-pit! As a batsman, he was a powerful hitter, favouring the off-drive, but also had a solid defence that was characterised by great determination. He twice came as high as third in the national averages.

Unfortunately, Iddison was involved in a dispute which erupted at the North against South match in 1862. He was sufficiently piqued to not play a full part in the fixture list for seven years and in 1864 even sent his brother to play in his place in a game at The Oval, where the dispute had begun. Meanwhile the official County Club had been formed and Iddison led the team in its first match – against Surrey at The Oval starting on 4 June 1863. Later in the season his career best bowling figures helped the new outfit to an eight-wicket win. The first first-class century of his career came in 1866 – for Lancashire! It was that county's first-ever century.

In this early period of inter-county fixtures there were many versions of deciding the County Champions; however, it was generally accepted that Yorkshire, under Iddison's leadership, were the winners in 1867 and again three years later. As a leader, he was a shrewd judge of the game and handled his men effectively, although he could be quick-tempered at times. His all-round skills were backed-up by his fine fielding, in which he excelled at point. Following the end of his career Iddison continued to be involved in arranging matches, including for Lord Londesborough in the early days of the Scarborough Festival. He was without doubt a man of much influence; he held sway over the playing development of the very first years of Yorkshire CCC and laid the groundwork for its future successes.

Ray Illingworth

RHB and OB, 1951-1983

Full Name: Raymond Illingworth, CBE
Birth: Pudsey, 08/06/1932

Type of Player: Middle order right-hand batsman, right-arm off-break bowler

First Class Career for Yorkshire:
Debut: v. Hampshire, Headingley, 1951
Matches: 496
Batting: 14,986 runs (Av. 27.90), 14 centuries.
Highest Score: 162 v. Indians, Bramall Lane, Sheffield, 1959
Bowling: 1,431 wkts (Av. 18.73), 5wi 79 times.
Best performance: 9-42 v. Worcestershire, Worcester, 1957
Fielding: 286 catches
Year of last match: 1983

Tests: 61, 1958-1973

Known throughout the 1960s as one of the shrewdest brains on the county circuit, the most significant move in the career of Ray Illingworth came at the end of that decade when he cut off his ties with Yorkshire. Winning the Ashes in Australia was certainly the high point of his long career, but spells as manager of Yorkshire and, later, England were marred by controversy and lack of success.

Another of Pudsey's famous cricketing sons, Illingworth moved with his family to Farsley and it was for that club's first XI that he was playing by the age of fifteen. He was a batsman who could bowl medium pace but after being seen experimenting with off-spin was asked to bowl some on a rain-affected pitch, took 5 for 5 and never looked back. By the time of his first 100-wicket haul, in 1956, Illingworth had developed into a very accurate off-spinner. He would bowl a nagging line and length and turn the ball appreciably, especially in helpful conditions. His slow-stepping run-up was merely the prelude to another teasing delivery and he was one of the few bowlers who was very rarely 'collared'.

For the first eleven years of his Test career his appearances were spasmodic but his best Test bowling figures came in 1967 when he took 6 for 29 against India at Lord's under the leadership of Close. 1959 was Illingworth's best season with the bat – 1,726 runs at 46.64, including five centuries – and he was a flamboyant stroke-maker in the earlier part of his career. Later, he settled into the number six position from where he was able to guide the course of the innings. He was just as capable of a determined defensive innings as one that kept the scoreboard moving. He also played a vital role in the brilliant fielding side of the 1960s, especially by taking several fine catches in the gully.

The best match of Illingworth's career, statistically, was against Kent at Dover in 1964. A knock of 135 was followed by 14 wickets – 7 in each innings. He had the remarkable figures of 7 for 6 against Gloucestershire at Harrogate in 1967 and was the country's leading wicket-taker in 1968 with 131 victims at 14.36. This remained his best season but it was his last with Yorkshire. He was refused a contract for longer than one year and Leicestershire made him an offer that included the captaincy.

Within weeks of joining his new county, Illingworth had become England captain. At first this was due to an injury to Colin

Left: *Batting practice for the youthful Ray Illingworth at Headingley in the 1950s.*
Right: *Illingworth bowling his off-spin in the Yorkshire nets.*

Cowdrey, but success meant that he was able to assume the mantle in his own right. He retained the position for five years and England lost only 5 of the 31 Tests for which he was in charge. His greatest effort was in winning the Ashes on Australian soil in 1970/71 and his determined approach was shown by both his batting and bowling averages improving after taking over the leadership. His highest Test innings was 113 against West Indies at Lord's in 1969.

He was also a very successful county captain, leading Leicestershire to the first trophies in their entire history – the County Championship in 1975 and two one-day trophies. He was outstanding at bringing out the best in all types of players at both county and national level and was fiercely loyal to them. It was therefore fully expected that he would do the same for Yorkshire on his return as manager for the 1979 season. However, five years of rankling off the field left Illingworth a deeply embittered man. He was recalled to the captaincy fifteen days after his fiftieth birthday in 1982 but the following season ignominiously led the side to bottom place in the Championship for the only time in its history. He was summarily sacked by a brand new committee swept into power on a wave of discontent.

Thus a playing career was concluded with 24,134 runs (average 28.06), 2,072 wickets (20.28) and 446 catches. In 212 limited-overs matches the totals were 2,349 runs and 181 wickets with a best of 5-29 in the victorious Gillette Cup final against Surrey in 1965, co-incidentally Illingworth's benefit year (which produced £6,604). He was one of the *Wisden* five for 1960.

In 1994, after a successful spell as a television commentator, he was persuaded to become England manager and this proved to be another unhappy period. It included an embarrassing performance in the 1996 World Cup as well as further disputes through his handling of some players and his lack of a modern approach. Illingworth was a vital component of Yorkshire's Championship-winning side of the 1960s but it remains frustrating that the greatest moments in his career came after he had left the county. What he might have achieved with Yorkshire's youngsters in the 1970s will never be known.

Stanley Jackson

RHB and RFM, 1890-1907

Full Name: Rt Hon. Sir Frank Stanley Jackson (also known as Francis Stanley Jackson)
Birth: Chapel Allerton, Leeds, 21/11/1870
Death: Knightsbridge, London, 09/03/1947

Type of Player: Middle order right-hand batsman, right-arm fast medium bowler

First Class Career for Yorkshire:
Debut: v. Lancashire, Huddersfield, 1890
Matches: 207
Batting: 10,371 runs (Av. 33.89), 21 centuries.
Highest Score: 160 v.Gloucestershire, Bramall Lane, Sheffield, 1898
Bowling: 506 wkts (Av. 19.15), 5wi 25 times.
Best performance: 7-42 v. Middlesex, Headingley, 1898
Fielding: 129 catches
Year of last match: 1907

Tests: 20, 1893-1905

To many people, Stanley Jackson epitomised the Golden Age of cricket. He was Yorkshire's most brilliant amateur, mixing panache with determination to produce an outstanding player and leader. Jackson led the Harrow XI in his final year. He gained his blue at Cambridge for each of four years, topping both batting and bowling averages in 1892 when he was captain. He also led in 1893 and was involved in controversy when he allowed one of his bowlers to bowl wide so that Oxford would save the compulsory follow-on. After his first two Tests, he declined to play in the third, preferring to play for Yorkshire and it was felt that he might have gained the England captaincy earlier, had it not been for these two events.

One of the most natural cricketers of his era, Jackson was a consistent all-rounder. He batted in an orthodox manner and had a solid technique allied to excellent timing and brilliant strokes, especially the on-drive. When bowling he controlled his variations skillfully and used the off-cutter effectively. 1899 was his best season with the bat (1,947 runs at 45.04) but also a year when he was passed over for the England captaincy. After a break for military service, Jackson returned to the Test scene in 1902 and was England's best batsman, making significant contributions especially after collapses. Not content with that, he helped his county bowl out the Australians for 23 by taking 5 for 12. The England captaincy was now his to take and he was asked to lead the 1903/04 side to Australia; sadly he declined because of business commitments.

The year 1905 will forever be known as 'Jackson's Year'. Leading his country against Australia, he won all five tosses, the series two-nil and came top of both batting and bowling averages. The best score of his Test career, 144 not out, was Headingley's first such century and no Ashes captain has ever bettered his series bowling average of 15.46. As a leader he was always firm and clear, did not consult much and remained unruffled in a crisis. Following his playing career he served as MCC president, Test selector – twice chairman – and was Yorkshire president at the time of his death. Sir Stanley Jackson was the authentic amateur of the Golden Age. He loved the game and played it with flair and style. The Australians knew he also played it with steel.

Paul Jarvis

RHB and RFM, 1981-1993

Full Name: Paul William Jarvis
Birth: Redcar, 29/06/1965

Type of Player: Lower order right-hand batsman, right-arm fast medium bowler

First Class Career for Yorkshire:
Debut: v. Sussex, Hove, 1981
Matches: 138
Batting: 1,898 runs (Av. 16.64). Highest Score: 80 v. Northamptonshire, Scarborough, 1992
Bowling: 449 wkts (Av. 26.70), 5wi 18 times. Best performance: 7-55 v. Surrey, Headingley, 1986
Fielding: 36 catches
Year of last match: 1993

Tests: 9, 1987/88-1992/93

The career of Paul Jarvis must be one of the most frustrating in Yorkshire's history. The county's youngest-ever debutante was dubbed the 'fastest white bowler in the world' by Peter Roebuck at the time of his first Test, yet his eventual departure from his county was marked with relief rather than regret.

Jarvis made his first-class debut at the tender age of 16 years and 75 days. He developed gradually through the remainder of his teens but Yorkshire's yearning for a quality fast bowler meant that he was possibly over-used at his relatively young age. Even so, by 1986, he was able to take over 50 wickets for the first time and the following season was his best-ever, with 81 wickets at an average of 24.58.

Despite not being particularly tall for a fast bowler, Jarvis had developed an action that made the ball skid through at a good pace. His yorker was his prize ball and was particularly effective in demolishing the tail in limited-overs matches. Pace in itself was not enough at Test level, however, and he had a particularly chastening experience at the hands of Australia's Steve Waugh at Lord's in 1989. 1988 had been the first year when lengthy lay-offs through injuries had reared their ugly heads. Nevertheless, Jarvis still topped the Yorkshire bowling, though playing in only five matches, taking his 31 victims at only 14 runs each.

With this mixed record and an uncertain international future, he went on the ill-fated unofficial tour to South Africa in 1989/90 and patience amongst the Yorkshire public started to wear thin after only four appearances in 1991. Two more years of intermittent injuries were enough and he joined Sussex for the 1994 season. After five years he moved to Somerset and has now taken 647 wickets (av 29.02) in first-class matches.

Jarvis took 209 wickets (average 21.89) in limited-overs matches for Yorkshire with a best of 6 for 27 against Somerset at Taunton in 1989. His 24 wickets in 16 one-day internationals included 5 for 35 against India at Bangalore in 1992/93. So what went wrong? Was his stocky frame not up to the rigours of bowling the great pace demanded regularly? For Jarvis to play for the county at such a young age and not fulfill his potential makes this one of Yorkshire's saddest personal stories.

Roy Kilner

LHB and SLA, 1911-1927

Full Name: Roy Kilner
Birth: Low Valley, Wombwell, 17/10/1890
Death: Kendray, Barnsley, 05/04/1928

Type of Player: Middle order left-hand batsman, slow left-arm bowler

First Class Career for Yorkshire:
Debut: v. Somerset, Taunton, 1911
Matches: 365
Batting: 13,018 runs (Av. 30.13), 15 centuries.
Highest Score: 206* v. Derbyshire, Bramall Lane, Sheffield, 1920
Bowling: 857 wkts (Av. 17.33), 5wi 39 times.
Best performance: 8-26 v. Glamorgan, Cardiff Arms Park, 1923
Fielding: 231 catches
Year of last match: 1927

Tests: 9, 1924-1926

Aptly described as 'the Friar Tuck of the Yorkshire team', Roy Kilner can lay claim to being one of the most popular and cherished cricketers ever to wear the white rose cap. With his long chin, merry eyes and cap askew he was a generous, modest character; a man of rare charm and humour.

Life for Kilner began in Wombwell, near Barnsley. A nephew of Irving Washington, a stylish left-handed batsman who played 44 matches for Yorkshire, Kilner played for local side Mitchell Main and was in the Yorkshire second team by 1910. His brother Norman was also destined for a career in county cricket, mainly with Warwickshire. Pre-war, Kilner played four seasons for Yorkshire chiefly as an aggressive left-handed batsman whose favourite strokes were the off-drive and pull. His best season as a batsman was 1913, when he scored 1,586 runs at 34.47, one of ten occasions when he exceeded 1,000 runs during a summer.

The loss of his good friend Major Booth in World War One and the death of Alonzo Drake brought new responsibilities for Kilner in the 1920s. He developed into a true all-round player for the county. Four times he completed the 'double', with a best of 1,404 runs and 158 wickets in 1923. His nagging bowling with its variations of pace and flight made him a vital component of Yorkshire's Championship-winning side of the early 1920s, and in 1924 he was selected as one of *Wisden*'s Five Bowlers of the Year. Kilner toured Australia in 1924/25, assisting in England's Test victory at Melbourne scoring 74 and taking 5 for 70 in the match. He also toured the West Indies in 1925/26 and in total played 9 times for England.

Above all else though, Kilner is best remembered for his enduring sense of fun even during the stern conflict of a Roses encounter: 'We says good morning and after that the only thing we says is "How's that?"'. He became one of the most easily recognised county cricketers during the 1920s, with his broad round face and solid appearance. His easy disposition won him friends wherever he went. Enteric fever, contracted during a coaching trip to India in 1927/28, claimed him at the age of only thirty-seven. It is estimated that around 100,000 people crowded the streets of Wombwell for Kilner's funeral. Later *Wisden* wrote: 'Few modern professionals commanded such a measure of esteem and kindly regard from his own immediate colleagues and opponents in the cricket field as did Roy Kilner.'

Eddie Leadbeater

RHB and LB, 1949-1956

Full Name: Edric Leadbeater
Birth: Lockwood, Huddersfield, 15/08/1927

Type of Player: Lower order right-hand batsman, right-arm leg-break bowler

First Class Career for Yorkshire:
Debut: v. Leicestershire, Grace Road, Leicester, 1949
Matches: 81
Batting: 898 runs (Av. 13.81). Highest Score: 91 v. Nottinghamshire, Bramall Lane, Sheffield, 1951
Bowling: 201 wkts (Av. 28.14), 5wi 7 times. Best performance: 8-83 v. Worcestershire, Worcester, 1950
Fielding: 49 catches
Year of last match: 1956

Tests: 2, 1951/52

The art of leg-break bowling has never had strong roots in Yorkshire cricket. One of the few exponents to have represented the county was Eddie Leadbeater, who never won a county cap yet played twice for England. Huddersfield-born, Leadbeater was a professional at Almondbury at the age of seventeen. A short (5 ft, 6 in) lively bowler, he was slow in pace, gave the ball plenty of flight and varied his deliveries, using the odd top-spinner rather than the googly.

In only his second season with Yorkshire he captured 87 first-class wickets, during the wet summer of 1950, at an average of less than 27 apiece. His 8 for 83 at Worcester that same season remains the best innings figures by a Yorkshire leg-break bowler. *The Cricketer* endorsed Leadbeater's achievements that year, recording: 'The discovery of the season was undoubtedly Leadbeater with his leg breaks. Thus he caused a break with tradition. For years Yorkshire have had no need of a leg-break bowler. Famous left-handers of the past had provided the wristy spin in that direction. Leadbeater was the personality of the side and his fielding too made him indispensable.'

A tally of 66 county wickets in 1951 included seven in one innings against Nottinghamshire and that winter he was flown out to India to replace the injured A.E.G. Rhodes. He took 20 first-class wickets on the tour and played in two Tests where his 2 wickets cost him 109 runs each – he was never chosen again for England. Thereafter his form declined and, unable to command a regular place in the Yorkshire side, he moved to Warwickshire after the 1956 season.

A more-than-useful late order batsman, his only first-class hundred (116) was scored against Glamorgan at Coventry in 1958 going in as 'nightwatchman'. It was his final season of county cricket. Back in Huddersfield league cricket, he went on to break numerous bowling records, surpassing Walter Bedford's tally of 1,346 wickets in 1974. For his club, Almondbury, he dominated the 1962 Sykes Cup final, scoring a century and taking four wickets, not to mention three catches. Leadbeater's 201 wickets for Yorkshire was an ultimately modest career return after the promise of 1950. But he remains the last such specialist to represent the county and his 'skilful combination of flight and spin' at Worcester ensured a rare moment of glory for a Yorkshire leg-break bowler.

Ted Lester

RHB and OB, 1945-1956

Full Name: Edward Ibson Lester
Birth: Scarborough, 18/02/1923

Type of Player: Middle order right-hand batsman, right-arm off-break bowler

First Class Career for Yorkshire:
Debut: v. RAF, Scarborough, 1945
Matches: 228
Batting: 10,616 runs (Av. 34.02), 24 centuries. Highest Score: 186 v Warwickshire, Scarborough, 1949
Bowling: 3 wkts (Av. 53.33). Best performance: 1-7 v. Essex, Southend, 1947
Fielding: 106 catches
Year of last match: 1956

Tests: Nil

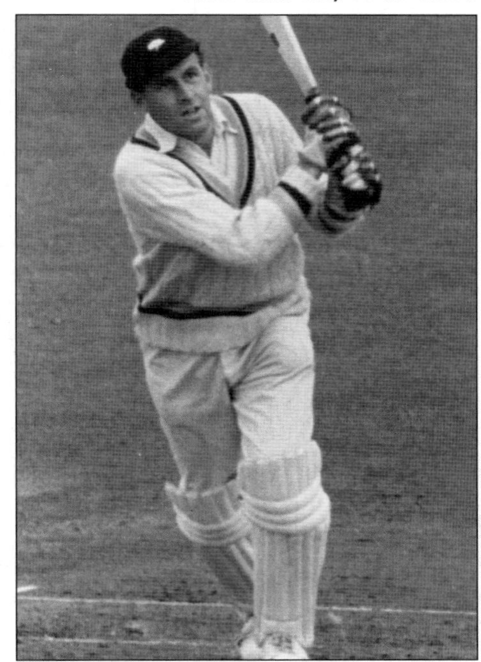

One of the stalwarts of the county scene for over forty-five years, Ted Lester served Yorkshire mainly as player, Second XI captain and scorer but also in several unofficial capacities as well. He always put the interests of the club first. Lester attended the Headingley nets in 1939, but for the next few years his playing activities were confined to club level. He had scored prolifically on the batsman's paradise at North Marine Road and this ensured that he was first in line for a place in the county side when it was rebuilt after the war. He first played for Yorkshire in friendly games but began to appear more regularly when the County Championship was resumed in 1946.

The number four position was made Lester's own and he usually scored at a good speed. Although his methods were somewhat unorthodox, he was dangerous when set and could change the course of a game in a short period of time. He was well co-ordinated and especially strong on the leg side, his method being based on a quick eye. Although he had the ability to hit the ball hard with little effort, his late cut was, in contrast, a delightful stroke. The fine summer of 1947 brought out the best in Lester and he averaged 73, his record including three consecutive centuries.

His highest aggregate (1,801 runs at 37.52) came in 1949, but soon after entering his thirties a foot problem started to restrict him somewhat and he lost form after the 1954 season. Being dropped to the second team did have its compensation, however, as it was soon realised that his paternal nature would make him an ideal colts leader. This he became, and fulfilled the position for four seasons from 1958. The team won the Minor Counties Championship in his first campaign and never finished lower than fifth under his captaincy.

Lester's third career with Yorkshire was his longest. For thirty-one seasons he travelled with the first team, officially as scorer, but also as someone who could always be approached for advice or information. He was present only at home games for his last few years and finally put down his pencil at the age of sixty-nine. A testimonial in 1956 produced £3,000 for Lester but no amount could ever be appropriate for someone who passed on wisdom and experience in such large and widely-appreciated measures.

Maurice Leyland

LHB and SLA, 1920-1946

Full Name: Morris Leyland (known as Maurice)
Birth: New Park, Harrogate, 20/07/1900
Death: Scotton Banks, Knaresborough, 01/01/1967

Type of Player: Middle order left-hand batsman, slow left-arm bowler

First Class Career for Yorkshire:
Debut: v. Essex, Southend, 1920
Matches: 548
Batting: 26,181 runs (Av. 41.03), 62 centuries.
Highest Score: 263 v. Essex, Anlaby Road, Hull, 1936
Bowling: 409 wkts (Av. 27.08), 5wi 10 times.
Best performance: 8-63 v. Hampshire, Fartown, Huddersfield, 1938
Fielding: 204 catches
Year of last match: 1946

Tests: 41, 1928-1938

Dependable and solid, Maurice Leyland was one of Yorkshire and England's best left-handed batsmen. He relished a battle and no cause was too great for his broad shoulders to bear. Behind the courage and pluck though there was great enthusiasm and humour. Born in Harrogate, Leyland's Christian name was registered as Morris but he was always known as 'Maurice'. His father – at one time the groundsman at Headingley – started him off as a cricketer at Moorside in Lancashire. By the age of eighteen he was playing with his home club, Harrogate, and in 1920 made his county entrance.

The youthful Leyland took some time to develop but having obtained the security of his Yorkshire cap in 1922, his play progressed significantly thereafter. In 1923 he reached 1,000 runs in a season for the first time. In the seventeen seasons that followed, to 1939, he did not fail to pass that particular landmark and three times extended his run tally passed 2,000. The first of five double centuries was made in 1927 at Bramall Lane in the match with Middlesex, although his highest first-class score came nine years later. He still shares three of Yorkshire's record wicket partnerships – 346 for the second wicket with Barber in 1932, 323 unbeaten with Sutcliffe for the third wicket in 1928 and, for the sixth wicket, 276 with Emmott Robinson in 1926. As a batsman he could not claim the grace of a Woolley or a Gower, but he was immensely effective with his wide stance and powerful strokes. R.C. Robertson-Glasgow wrote in *Wisden* in 1943: 'Leyland has always stood very still at the crease, whether waiting for the bowler or watching the striker; there is no fuss, no fidget; there is no nervous adjusting of pads or gloves, no jerky talk with the umpire or fieldsman. He has a task and its answer, and he addresses himself to it, broad-bottomed, straight-eyed, with the forearms of a blacksmith, yet nimble, strangely nimble of foot.'

Despite his consistency, it took the England selectors until Leyland's eighth season of first-class cricket before rewarding him with a Test cap. A poor start – dismissed for nought – against the West Indies, did not prevent him from being chosen to tour Australia under Percy Chapman that winter. In 1928 he scored 1,783 first-class runs and was duly recognised by *Wisden* in 1929, who selected him amongst the Five Cricketers of the Year. He confirmed his ability at the highest level, scoring the first of his nine Test hundreds (seven against Australia), in the Fifth Test of that Ashes series at Melbourne.

He toured Australia three times; in addition to the 1928/29 visit he played his part fully in the 'bodyline' series of 1932/33 and under 'Gubby' Allen in 1936/37. His record against the 'old enemy', both home and away, is special. In 20 of his 41 Tests matches he scored 1,705 runs at an average of 56.83. In Leyland's final Test at The Oval in 1938, he scored 187, sharing a second-wicket partnership of 382 with Len Hutton in England's Test record score of 903 for 7 declared. The Yorkshire left-hander thus became the first to score hundreds in his first and last innings against Australia, a feat somewhat overshadowed by his young county colleague's 364. A final Test record of 2,764 runs at 46.06 placed Leyland in the highest class as a Test batsman.

A brilliant outfielder, Leyland excelled in the deep where, despite his stocky physique, he covered the ground quickly with a clean pick up and swift return to the wicket. Rhodes and Roy Kilner, as Yorkshire's premier slow left-arm bowlers, limited Leyland's chances in that department; however, his mixture of left arm 'chinaman' and googlies, bowled with a broad smile, brought him 466 first-class wickets at 29 each including a hat-trick at Sheffield in 1935 against Surrey. Examples of Leyland's character and humour thankfully are engraved in the annals of Yorkshire cricket. When debating how to deal with quick bowlers he coined an historic phrase, captured by Neville Cardus: 'None of us like fast bowlers, only some of us don't let on.' Comparing the boisterous Sydney spectators with his native Yorkshire crowds he commented: 'They should coom to Sheffield on Bank Holiday and hear t'crowd there. Why, compared to them, these folks on t'hill sounded to me as 'armonious as t'Uddersfield Choral Society.'

After the war he helped Yorkshire to capture the twelfth Championship title of his career and his final appearance in first-class cricket was in 1948, when he became a life member of Yorkshire CCC. His serene and cheerful outlook endeared him to the young players he coached at Yorkshire in the 1950s and 1960s, in contrast to Arthur Mitchell's rather forthright approach. In the closing years of his life he battled with Parkinson's disease, displaying the same fortitude that so characterised his cricket. Admired wherever he went, Leyland displayed the true spirit and strength required to earn respect and success for both county and country, as E.M. Wellings noted: 'There was no more stirring sight in cricket than that of Maurice Leyland going out to bat when his side was in difficulties. His short, square figure advancing to the wicket exuded confidence.'

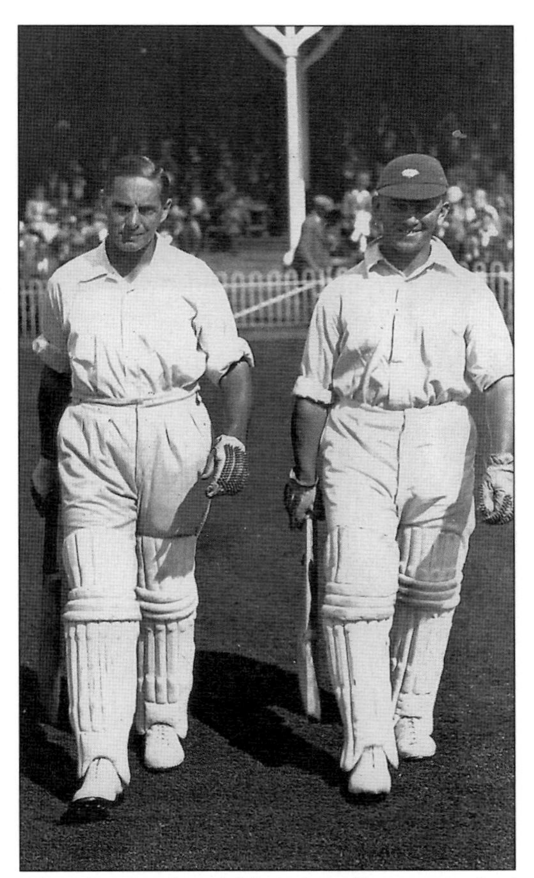

Maurice Leyland (right) walks out to bat with Herbert Sutcliffe for Yorkshire, against the MCC at Scarborough in 1934.

Ephraim Lockwood

RHB and RM, 1868-1884

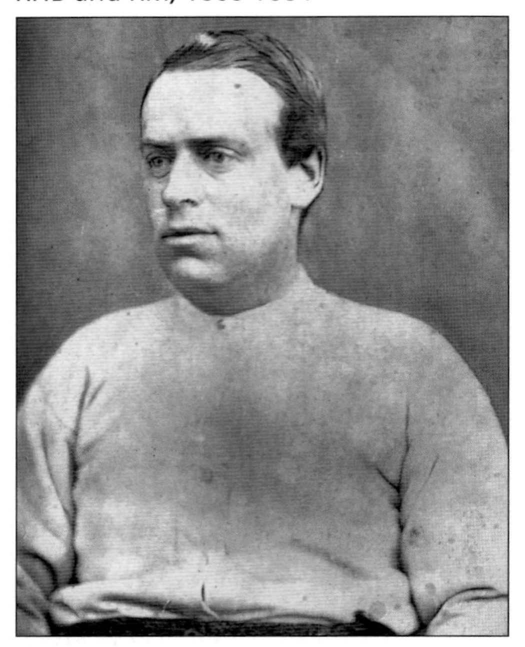

Full Name: Ephraim Lockwood*
Birth: Lascelles Hall, Huddersfield, 04/04/1845
Death: Tandem, Lascelles Hall, 19/12/1921

Type of Player: Opening/middle order right-hand batsman, slow medium right-arm bowler

First Class Career for Yorkshire:
Debut: v. Surrey, The Oval, 1868
Matches: 213
Batting: 7,758 runs (Av. 23.22), 6 centuries.
Highest Score: 208 v. Kent, Gravesend, 1883
Bowling: 135 wkts (Av. 16.49), 5wi 3 times.
Best performance: 6-26 v. Middlesex, Bramall Lane, Sheffield, 1875
Fielding: 163 catches, 2 stumpings
Year of last match: 1884

Tests: Nil

The village of Lascelles Hall, near Huddersfield, provided a number of the county's earliest champions, one of which was Ephraim Lockwood. An unassuming, uneducated, parochial type, he played for Yorkshire between 1868 and 1884 and was amongst the best batsmen of his generation. His love of the game stemmed from his early days at Lascelles Hall when he recalled: 'I have occasionally dined on a turnip rather than break away from a good practice.'

Lockwood's remarkable first appearance for the county has become part of Yorkshire cricket folklore. Called to The Oval as a late replacement, he made his debut against Surrey, opening the batting with his uncle John Thewlis, who had recommended his nephew. Ridiculed and mocked by the Oval spectators for his appearance – a green, black and red check shirt, short trousers and ill fitting boots – Lockwood (91) shared an opening stand with Thewlis (108) of 176 and Yorkshire won by an innings.

His strength as a batsman lay in his ability to play the cut shot, often played off middle stump, which the Nottingham premier batsman Richard Daft described as 'simply perfection'. For Yorkshire he quickly became one of the mainstays of the side. He hit 1,000 runs in a season four times, with a best of 1,261 at 32.33 in 1876.

His only double century was made at Gravesend against Kent in 1883. The previous season his benefit brought him £591. Lockwood's stature as a batsman brought several invitations to tour Australia which he turned down, although he did make the trip to North America in 1879. He did not enjoy the attention of the mosquitoes and on a visit to Niagara Falls, when asked what he thought of the glorious sight, he replied: 'If this is the Falls of Niagara, I'd sooner be at Lascelles Hall.' When the Australians toured England in 1878 they considered Lockwood to have more strokes than any other English batsmen except of course the 'Champion' W.G. Grace.

His easy-going, phlegmatic approach perhaps did not make him the ideal candidate to captain a Yorkshire side that contained some fierce temperaments and outspoken characters and his two seasons as the county's leader were undistinguished. Married twice, his second wife was the niece of the famous Kent batsman Fuller Pilch. Lockwood died in December 1921. The finest batsman of the club's formative years, his cut shot, 'like a flash behind point', remained his lasting epitaph.

Jim Love

RHB and RM, 1975-1989

Full Name: James Derek Love
Birth: Headingley, Leeds, 22/04/1955

Type of Player: Middle order right-hand batsman, right-arm medium pace bowler

First Class Career for Yorkshire:
Debut: v. Derbyshire, Chesterfield, 1975
Matches: 247
Batting: 10,263 runs (Av. 31.10), 13 centuries. Highest Score: 170* v. Worcestershire, Worcester, 1979
Bowling: 12 wkts (Av. 69.58). Best performance: 2-0 v. Windward Islands, St Lucia, 1986/87
Fielding: 123 catches
Year of last match: 1989

Tests: Nil

The high point of Jim Love's career was at Lord's on 11 July 1987. He blocked the last ball, from West Indian Winston Davis, of the Benson & Hedges Cup final and Yorkshire (244-6) had won its first one-day final for eighteen years. The scores had finished level but Northamptonshire (244-7) had lost more wickets. Not only that but the hero Love finished on 75 not out and won the Gold Award for his outstanding innings.

Love played his early cricket for Kirkstall Educational and Leeds and captained the Yorkshire Federation team in 1974. He made his debut for Yorkshire as a young, hard-hitting batsman but never really established himself as a permanent fixture in the team for first-class matches. He played several attacking innings in one-day cricket and was rewarded, in 1981, by appearances in three one-day internationals. He remains the only Yorkshire player to have performed in such matches without ever playing Test cricket.

Love was powerful and strong, but also easy-going and it is possible that with a greater sense of determination he might have fulfilled the obvious promise that he showed. He was more than capable of accelerating the scoring and was well-suited to the number four position in which he usually found himself. His best forcing shot was the drive, especially square or through the covers, which he struck with considerable power.

Love's best season was 1983, when he scored 1,203 runs (average 33.41). His 4,298 runs in limited-overs matches for the county include four centuries and over 1,000 runs in the Benson & Hedges Cup alone. His best score of 118 not out was achieved twice – against Scotland at Bradford in 1981 and against Surrey at Headingley in 1987.

His benefit, which realised £92,000, came in his final season. Three seasons with Lincolnshire were followed by a significant move to Scotland. Appointed coach, he continued to play, especially in limited-overs matches, and later helped steer the country to its first World Cup finals in 1999. Despite losing all five games, the team gave a favourable impression and there is no doubt that Love is at the forefront of the development of the game north of the border. Love continues to give his best to the game. His positive approach as a player is being instilled in his charges and if anyone can repeat his effort of 1987, he will be a hero indeed.

Frank Lowson

RHB and OB, 1949-1958

Full Name: Frank Anderson Lowson
Birth: Bradford, 01/07/1925
Death: Pool-in-Wharfedale, 08/09/1984

Type of Player: Opening right-hand batsman, right-arm off-break bowler

First Class Career for Yorkshire:
Debut: v. Cambridge University, Fenner's, 1949
Matches: 252
Batting: 13,897 runs (Av. 37.25), 30 centuries.
Highest Score: 259* v. Worcestershire, Worcester, 1953
Bowling: 0 wkts
Fielding: 180 catches
Year of last match: 1958

Tests: 7, 1951-1955

Frank Lowson was one of the famous triumvirate, with Close and Trueman, who all made their first-class debuts at the same time. Lowson became a reliable and very watchable opening partner for Hutton. Sadly he suffered from poor health; otherwise he might well have played several more times for England. Lowson showed so much promise that he played for Bradford Grammar School First XI at the age of eleven, and his first club was Bowling Old Lane.

He soon proved with Yorkshire that he had the ideal temperament for an opening batsman and his technique, being based on a solid defence, appeared to be near perfect. He was well-organised in his stroke-play, especially in cutting and driving, and the comparisons with Hutton were always most complimentary. It was even said by Trueman that watching the pair in full flow from a distance, it was sometimes difficult to distinguish between them. Lowson took part in 44 century opening stands for Yorkshire; 22 of these were with Hutton and a further 10 with Halliday. He scored 58 on his Test debut (at Headingley) against South Africa, his stand with Hutton being worth a tantalising 99 on this occasion. He toured India in 1951/52 and made his best Test score of 68 at Delhi. He had six different opening partners in his all-too-brief career at the highest level.

Lowson was of slim build, almost frail and suffered considerably from varicose veins, which led to premature retirement. The county was dominated by strong personalities behind the scenes and when he was approached later in life about his experiences in the Yorkshire dressing room he declined to be drawn into conversation. He was quiet and unassuming and J.M. Kilburn felt that, at Test level, he lacked the necessary drive and ambition.

However, the picture is certainly not one of under-achievement on the county scene. Lowson passed 1,000 runs in a season nine times, including in India, and his best season was as early in his career as 1950; he scored 2,152 runs (average 42.19). His highest innings, three years later, was his only double-century. His testimonial, in 1959, realised £2,500. Sympathy and sadness are the feelings evoked by Lowson. He met a relatively early death and his career did not quite touch the heights which it had promised, but those who watched him bat knew that they had seen a quality player.

Richard Lumb

RHB and RM, 1970-1984

Full Name: Richard Graham Lumb
Birth: Doncaster, 27/02/1950

Type of Player: Opening right-hand batsman, right-arm medium pace bowler

First Class Career for Yorkshire:
Debut: v. Worcestershire, Worcester, 1970
Matches: 239
Batting: 11,525 runs (Av. 31.57), 22 centuries. Highest Score: 165* v. Gloucestershire, Park Avenue, Bradford, 1984
Bowling: 0 wkts
Fielding: 129 catches
Year of last match: 1984

Tests: Nil

Another in Yorkshire's long line of fine opening batsmen, Richard Lumb found himself with the unenviable task of being Boycott's regular partner throughout most of his career. That he had considerable success in this capacity was due to his professionalism and solidity.

Lumb was grandson of Joe Lumb (founder of the competition which bears that name) and attended school in Mexborough and Doncaster. He captained Yorkshire Under-15s and played club cricket for Brodsworth Main. In 1968 he scored a double century for ESCA and won two league junior batting awards. Much, therefore, was expected of him. Lumb scored his first century for Yorkshire in 1973 in a Roses match at Old Trafford when conditions were not entirely in the batsman's favour.

He was a tall, elegant player who specialised in the drive, mainly straight and through the covers. He played in two Test trials and commentators have felt that he lacked the necessary resolve to become an England player. Others have excused him on account of the fact that his technique may have suffered through having to play different types of cricket. It is also pointed out that he had much ability at slip but often lacked concentration. The difficulties under which Yorkshire played their cricket for most of his career must have been a factor and this may have influenced his decision to turn down the captaincy when it was offered.

Nevertheless, Lumb proved an ideal partner for Boycott. His good technique, courage and temperament meant that they could stand up well together, particularly against the overseas fast bowlers, of which the county had no equivalent. Their partnership accrued 10,458 runs in first-class matches – more than any other pair since 1945 – at an average of 48.19. Their record of 29 century partnerships is exceeded only by Holmes and Sutcliffe and their best was 288 against Somerset at Harrogate in 1979. Lumb's best season was 1975 when he scored 1,532 runs (average 41.40), finishing second in the county averages for Yorkshire.

His 1983 benefit brought him £50,235 and by this time he had spent several winters coaching in South Africa. This resulted in him meeting his wife and emigrating on retirement. Perhaps Lumb did not fulfill his promise. However, he was a reliable opener through a difficult time and an inconsistent batting line-up could rely on him more often than not.

George Macaulay

RHB and RFM/OB, 1920-1935

Full Name: George Gibson Macaulay
Birth: Thirsk, 07/12/1897
Death: Sullom Voe, Shetland Islands, 13/12/1940

Type of Player: Lower order right-hand batsman, right-arm fast medium/off-break bowler

First Class Career for Yorkshire:
Debut: v. Derbyshire, Bramall Lane, Sheffield, 1920
Matches: 445
Batting: 5,717 runs (Av. 17.97), 3 centuries.
Highest Score: 125* v. Nottinghamshire, Trent Bridge, 1921
Bowling: 1,774 wkts (Av. 17.22), 5wi 125 times.
Best performance: 8-21 v. Indians, Harrogate, 1932
Fielding: 361 catches
Year of last match: 1935

Tests: 8, 1922/23-1933

In sheer intensity of approach, George Macaulay was one of the most aggressive spin bowlers in the history of the game. He was a lynchpin of the post-1918 Yorkshire side and took a host of wickets on their behalf. At Barnard Castle School, and in club cricket with Thirsk Victoria and Ossett, he bowled at a fast pace but lack of early success with the county side resulted in some advice from Hirst. The consequence of this was that he slowed down and started to give the ball some sharp turn. This meant that he could be utilised in a versatile capacity, opening the bowling with lethal swing and later turning to off-spin. This change transformed his career and from the start of the 1921 season Macaulay never lost his place in the side.

Although not regarded as a true all-rounder his batting was certainly useful. When trouble occurred he would often succeed with precious runs earned through his fighting temperament. The 1922 season was the first of four consecutive Championship victories for Yorkshire and the leading wicket-taker for this period was Macaulay with 604 at 13.46. He took 6 for 8 at Northampton in 1922, when only three scoring strokes came from his 69 deliveries! He toured South Africa the following winter and took 16 wickets in his first four Test matches, including one with his very first ball! This was at Cape Town and he was also the hero at the end of the game, when he scored the winning hit in a cliff-hanging, one-wicket victory.

Although Macaulay topped the national averages in 1924, resulting in selection as one of *Wisden*'s Five Bowlers of the Year, his best campaign came the following year when he took 211 wickets (average 15.48). He formed a formidable pairing with Emmott Robinson and in 1927 Macaulay took 12 for 50 when the duo bowled unchanged against Worcestershire at Headingley. His benefit season came in 1931, but the resulting £1,633 was regarded by *Wisden* as 'small reward' for his long and untiring service. A total of 24 Test wickets was little to show for such a talented bowler.

It was suggested that Macaulay's outspoken nature may have contributed to lack of consistent selection and that his particularly hostile approach did not endear him to the authorities. His record, however, stands comparison with all the great practitioners of his era. His methods and style were highly successful and he was a vital player in a great side.

Ashley Metcalfe

RHB and OB, 1983-1995

Full Name: Ashley Anthony Metcalfe
Birth: Horsforth, Leeds, 25/12/1963

Type of Player: Opening right-hand batsman, right-arm off-break bowler

First Class Career for Yorkshire:
Debut: v. Nottinghamshire, Park Avenue, Bradford, 1983
Matches: 184
Batting: 10,465 runs (Av. 35.11), 25 centuries. Highest Score: 216* v. Middlesex, Headingley, 1988
Bowling: 3 wkts (Av. 114.66). Best performance: 2-18 v. Warwickshire, Scarborough, 1987
Fielding: 72 catches
Year of last match: 1995

Tests: Nil

One of the most attractive of Yorkshire's batsmen, Ashley Metcalfe will be best remembered for some exciting innings in limited-overs cricket and forging a successful opening partnership with Moxon in both forms of the game. Educated at Bradford Grammar School, Metcalfe played club cricket with Esholt and Farsley. He made an immediate impact in the Yorkshire side, with 122 in his debut innings and a stand of 248 with Boycott. His maiden limited-overs century came in the following season, with 115 not out against Gloucestershire at Scarborough. Two years later he had a brilliant season in the first-class game, scoring six centuries and coming close to being selected for the England tour of Australia.

In 1987 he scored more runs in limited-overs matches than any other batsman in the country and won four Gold Awards in Yorkshire's Benson & Hedges Cup-winning campaign. The highlight of this was when he and Moxon made a 211-run undefeated stand together to achieve a ten-wicket victory against Warwickshire at Edgbaston. Metcalfe liked to attack the new ball and had a natural flair for this, being stylish and adventurous. His *annus mirabilis* was 1990, when a fine summer and placid pitches enabled him to plunder 2,047 runs at 51.17. Against top-class bowlers, however, and on pitches which assisted the seam, his defence became a little suspect and this told on him in the end when he lost his place to the young Vaughan.

Moxon and Metcalfe scored 8,347 runs together when opening in first-class matches, their best stand being 282 against Lancashire at Old Trafford in 1986. Their 4,345 runs, average of 51.73 and 14 century stands in limited-overs matches are all Yorkshire records. Their best was against the bemused Warwickshire when they clocked up 242 and another ten-wicket win, this time at Headingley in the NatWest Trophy in 1990. On this occasion Metcalfe made his highest score of 127 not out and his final Yorkshire record in such games was 5,520 runs (average 32.09) with four centuries.

Metcalfe's release from Yorkshire came at the end of his benefit season, which raised £110,000. He had two years with Nottinghamshire and in 1999 scored a match-winning century for Cumberland in the Minor Counties Championship final. Although he may not have fulfilled his promise, Metcalfe's positive approach at the start of the innings often gave his county the momentum it needed. When in full flow his batting was truly exciting.

Frank Milligan

RHB and RF, 1894-1898

Full Name: Frank William Milligan
Birth: Farnborough, Hampshire, 19/03/1870
Death: Ramathlabama, Mafeking, South Africa, 31/03/1900

Type of Player: Middle/lower order right-hand batsman, right-arm fast bowler

First Class Career for Yorkshire:
Debut: v. Liverpool and District, Aigburth, 1894
Matches: 81
Batting: 1,879 runs (Av. 18.24). Highest Score: 74 v. Nottinghamshire, Trent Bridge, 1898
Bowling: 112 wkts (Av. 24.42), 5wi 3 times. Best performance: 7-65 v. Sussex, Bramall Lane, Sheffield, 1897
Fielding: 40 catches
Year of last match: 1898

Tests: 2, 1898/99

A typical carefree amateur cricketer of the late nineteenth century, Frank Milligan played only 81 times for his adopted county but was a popular player, respected by the 'pros' and, on his day, a wonderful hitter, quick bowler and talented fielder. Born in Farnborough, Hampshire while his father was serving in the Army at Aldershot, Milligan's only family link to Yorkshire was a great-grandmother from Rawdon.

His formative years were spent in south Derbyshire where his father had inherited Caldwell Hall. He learnt some cricket at Eton, although his early success came in Derbyshire village sides. Part of his father's inheritance was the Low Moor Iron Company near Bradford and, having entered the trade, Milligan became a member of the local club. By 1894 he was eligible to play for Yorkshire under the MCC two-year residential rule and he played his first match that same season.

Milligan was a late developer, but the more he played the better he became. A hard-hitting batsman, his top-score for Yorkshire was only 74 as his impatience and desire to score runs quickly prevented him achieving greater consistency. Lord Hawke considered Milligan's innings of 64 against Essex at Huddersfield in 1897 to be 'One of the finest instances of brilliant hitting I have ever watched'. As a bowler he was fast but erratic, as the *Athletic News* underlined in 1898: 'If he could get over his tendency to erratic deliveries, he would make a very dangerous fast bowler.' His best first-class figures, 7 for 61, were taken at Scarborough in 1898 for the Gentlemen against the Players. His fielding was perhaps more consistent than his batting or bowling.

He toured North America in 1895 and at the end of 1898 accepted an invitation from his county captain, Lord Hawke, to tour South Africa. His two Test appearances were unsuccessful, a top score of 38 at Cape Town his best. He remained wicketless but did take one brilliant boundary catch in the Second Test.

At the end of that tour, Milligan chose not to return to England but instead went to Bulawayo and gained a commission as a lieutenant in the Rhodesian Frontier Force. He was killed while serving with Colonel Plumer's troops, who were advancing on the Boer lines besieging Mafeking. A memorial sun-dial was erected to him in Harold Park, Low Moor as a lasting tribute both to his bravery and the cheerful, exuberant way he played his cricket.

Arthur Mitchell

RHB and SRA, 1922-1945

Full Name: Arthur Mitchell
Birth: Baildon Green, Bradford, 13/09/1902
Death: Bradford, 25/12/1976

Type of Player: Middle order right-hand batsman, right-arm slow bowler

First Class Career for Yorkshire:
Debut: v. Glamorgan, Headingley, 1922
Matches: 401
Batting: 18,189 runs (Av. 37.81), 39 centuries. Highest Score: 189 v. Northamptonshire, Northampton, 1926
Bowling: 5 wkts (Av. 58.20). Best performance: 3-49 v. Jamaica, Sabina Park, Kingston, 1936
Fielding: 406 catches
Year of last match: 1945

Tests: 6, 1933/34-1936

There have been few harder men in cricket than Arthur 'Ticker' Mitchell. A dogged, determined batsman, he applied the same firm and unbending approach as Yorkshire's coach after his playing days were over. Baildon Green was where the young Mitchell played his cricket. His county career got underway in 1922 but it was not until 1928, when he was capped, that he became a regular first team player. He served Yorkshire mainly at number three in the batting order, as the successor to Oldroyd.

A tenacious occupant of the crease, with a sound defensive technique, he was accused of carrying 'caution to excess' at times by accumulating his runs with on-side strokes, although he was capable of scoring quickly when needed. In 1933 he and Sutcliffe scored 105 in only 55 minutes at Bradford. His first century for the county remained his highest score in first-class cricket. He passed the 1,000 run mark in a season ten times and in 1933 scored 2,300 runs at 58.97 – including four successive centuries.

Mitchell met with little success on the tour to India (1933/34) but his effective style and appetite for a battle made him the ideal replacement for Leyland when he was called, from his garden, to play for England against South Africa at Leeds in 1935. He scored 58 and 72 in that match but his Test career was limited to just six appearances. He worked hard to become an exceptional close fielder. Mitchell was a specialist in the silly off and leg positions as well as a wonderful catcher at slip and gully, especially off Verity's bowling. He also liked to chatter constantly, a trait which earned him his enduring nickname of 'Ticker'.

He enjoyed a benefit in 1937, raising £2,227, and continued to play regularly up to the Second World War. In 1945 he became the county's coach and for the next quarter of a century worked hard to develop the young players at Headingley. He did not suffer fools gladly, and those whom he coached were left in no doubt about what Mitchell expected from them.

Mitchell's former county captain, Brian Sellers, paid tribute to him after he passed away on Christmas Day 1976: 'Arthur was a loyal supporter and hard worker for Yorkshire and he did extraordinary good work as a coach. He was a dedicated cricketer who worked hard at the game and became a resolute and determined player.' Fitting praise for a steel-like servant of Yorkshire cricket.

Frank Mitchell

RHB and RMF, 1894-1904

Full Name: Frank Mitchell
Birth: Market Weighton, 13/08/1872
Death: Blackheath, Kent, 11/10/1935

Type of Player: Middle order right-hand batsman, right-arm medium fast bowler

First Class Career for Yorkshire:
Debut: v. Gloucestershire, Headingley, 1894
Matches: 83
Batting: 4,104 runs (Av. 34.20), 10 centuries. Highest Score: 194 v. Leicestershire, Grace Road, Leicester, 1899
Bowling: 1 wkt (Av. 16.00). Best performance: 1-16 v. Worcestershire, Bramall Lane, Sheffield, 1899
Fielding: 52 catches
Year of last match: 1904

Tests: 2, 1898/99 (and 3, 1912, for South Africa)

A versatile sportsman, Frank Mitchell was a double-international in two senses of the term. He represented England at both cricket and rugby and played Test cricket for two different countries. After St Peter's School, York, Mitchell spent some time in Brighton, scoring heavily in club cricket and keeping goal for Sussex at soccer. He then went up to Cambridge and gained blues in three sports – cricket, rugby and putting the weight.

His 1894 first-class debut was for the varsity side against C.I. Thornton's XI and he later scored 75 and 92 against Yorkshire. He led Cambridge in 1896 but the Oxford game was marred by controversy. Wanting Oxford to bat last, he ordered one of his bowlers to concede extras so that his rivals could avoid the compulsory follow-on. Although the law was eventually changed, Mitchell suffered the indignity of having binoculars thrown at him and Oxford knocking off 330 to win by four wickets!

Although Mitchell's appearances for the county were spread over a period of eleven seasons, he only played for two full summers. The first of these was 1899, in which his record included seven half-centuries in twelve days, but the better one was 1901 when he scored 1,807 runs at 44.07. This included seven centuries, four of them coming in six innings.

He was a hard-hitting batsman, especially known for his off-side driving, and he scored at a good rate. Although not particularly stylish, he was aggressive, sound and could adapt his game to different types of pitch. His bowling was more useful for Cambridge than later in his career and his best figures – 5 for 57 – were for them against Surrey at The Oval in 1894. Both of Mitchell's Tests for England were in South Africa and he soon returned for the Boer War. He later settled there, playing for Transvaal and toured England twice as captain of his new country, the second occasion being in the only triangular Test tournament ever held in England. His success at the highest level was limited and he scored only 116 runs in his ten innings with a best of 41 at Cape Town in 1898/99.

As a rugby forward Mitchell played for England six times and his experience in so many sports enabled him to later follow a distinguished career as a sports journalist. There have been very few people able to write with such authority on so many sports.

Martyn Moxon

RHB and RM, 1981-1997

Full Name: Martyn Douglas Moxon
Birth: Stairfoot, Barnsley, 04/05/1960

Type of Player: Opening right-hand batsman, right-arm medium pace bowler

First Class Career for Yorkshire:
Debut: v. Essex, Headingley, 1981
Matches: 277
Batting: 18,973 runs (Av. 43.71), 41 centuries. Highest Score: 274* v. Worcestershire, Worcester, 1994
Bowling: 22 wkts (Av. 55.13). Best performance: 3-24 v. Hampshire, Southampton, 1989
Fielding: 190 catches
Year of last match: 1997

Tests: 10, 1986-1989

Tall and orthodox, with a sound technique, Martyn Moxon overcame some frightful injuries and bad luck off the field to firmly establish himself as one of Yorkshire's most stylish run scorers. Educated at Barnsley Holgate Grammar School, Moxon was coached by his father Derek and attended the well-known Wombwell Cricket Lovers' coaching classes. After playing for Monk Bretton, he went on to play for Barnsley, and later Bowling Old Lane. Progress was made through Yorkshire schools cricket and the Yorkshire Federation side and in 1979 he captained the England Under-19 side in Canada.

Making his first-class debut, he scored 116 against Essex, the first Yorkshire batsman to score a century on debut for sixty years. On 63 overnight, Moxon 'showed tremendous temperament and technique in his five-and-three-quarter-hour innings'. In the next home match at Abbeydale Park, Sheffield, Moxon became the first Yorkshireman to score centuries in his first two Championship matches. After such an auspicious start, his final average in his first season of county cricket was 27.26. He played only twice in 1982 and it was July before he got into the first team in 1983, but he again impressed with 153 in his first Roses match. It is reasonable to assume that the unhappiness in the Yorkshire dressing room hindered his early progress.

Awarded his county cap in May 1984, he repaid the club's commitment with 1,016 runs that summer, the first of eleven occasions that he passed the 1,000 run mark for Yorkshire. Picked by England for the Lord's Test against West Indies in June he was forced to withdraw with cracked ribs sustained during his innings of 90 on a difficult pitch at Northampton. He missed the next five matches but at the end of the season was selected for England's tour to India. He was forced to return home (although he later re-joined the tour) following the death of his father. The first of his ten Test caps finally came in 1986 and he made 74 on debut against New Zealand at Lord's.

Ill-fortune did overshadow Moxon's short Test career – 455 runs at 28.43. At Auckland on the 1987/88 tour of New Zealand he was dismissed for 99 having been stranded one short of his first Test century for eighteen minutes. Earlier, a sweep for three runs off Bracewell was wrongly signalled as leg-byes and so he became the fourth Yorkshire player to perish on 99. In the next Test at Wellington he was left 81 not out when rain

Martyn Moxon, one of Yorkshire's most stylish opening batsmen.

washed out the last two days of the match.

Ironically, his last England appearance in 1989 was followed by Moxon's best seasons in domestic cricket. He passed 1,600 runs for Yorkshire in both 1990 and 1991. The later season was his best and one of his most consistent, yielding 3 hundreds and 12 fifties. In the five seasons between 1990 and 1994 he scored 16 of his 41 centuries for Yorkshire. Opening the batting demands patience, and Moxon displayed that in abundance. His cover and off-drives were sweetly timed. There was power in his front and back foot play and above all a technical correctness was evident in all his shots – attack or defence. A useful right-arm medium pace bowler in his early county days, he was also an excellent slip fielder but later spent much of his time at mid-off or mid-on when the demands of captaincy came his way in 1990. There was also a requirement to protect his damaged fingers that did cause him several injury problems.

He led Yorkshire for six summers, from 1990 to 1995, but despite the arrival of an overseas player in the dressing room from 1992, success eluded Moxon's side. Eighth place in the Championship was the club's highest placing under his leadership. The highest of his five double centuries was 274 not out, made at Worcester in 1994. His benefit year, in the previous season, raised £103,000 and brought recognition from *Wisden* as a Cricketer of the Year in the 1993 edition. At Cardiff in 1996 he took part in the highest post-war opening stand for Yorkshire, of 362 against Glamorgan with Michael Vaughan, beating the 351 he and Boycott made against Worcestershire in 1985. His other major opening partner was Ashley Metcalfe, with whom he shared 21 century opening partnerships.

In addition to his almost 19,000 first-class runs for Yorkshire, Moxon made 7,307 one-day runs with a highest score of 141 not out at Sophia Gardens in 1991. Interestingly in the NatWest Trophy, the longer form of the one-day game, he averaged 47 with seven centuries. He also played eight one-day internationals for England.

Forced to retire in 1997 by a recurring back problem, he was appointed Yorkshire's first director of coaching later that year. During the winter of 1999/2000 he was chosen as coach of the England 'A' party that toured Bangladesh and New Zealand. Success in that role brought his appointment as assistant coach to the full national side for their one-day international fixtures in Kenya, Pakistan and Sri Lanka in 2000/2001. His sudden departure from Headingley in January 2001, to take up a position as first team coach at Durham CCC, came as a huge shock to many followers of Yorkshire cricket. Modest, unassuming and popular as a cricketer, Moxon at his classical best displayed the finest qualities of Yorkshire batsmanship.

Tony Nicholson

RHB and RMF, 1962-1975

Full Name: Anthony George Nicholson
Birth: Dewsbury, 25/06/1938
Death: Harrogate, 04/11/1985

Type of Player: Lower order right-hand batsman, right-arm medium fast bowler

First Class Career for Yorkshire:
Debut: v. Essex, Westcliff-on-Sea, 1962
Matches: 282
Batting: 1,667 runs (Av. 11.73). Highest Score: 50 v. Middlesex, Lord's, 1974
Bowling: 876 wkts (Av. 19.74), 5wi 40 times. Best performance: 9-62 v. Sussex, Eastbourne, 1967
Fielding: 85 catches
Year of last match: 1975

Tests: Nil

A right-arm medium pace bowler with good control and variety, Tony Nicholson was perhaps the best of Fred Trueman's many bowling partners for Yorkshire. Educated at Wheelwright Grammar School, Nicholson was originally a policeman and for five years followed his chosen occupation in what was then Rhodesia. Returning to England in the early 1960s, he gave up his job in 1961 to join Yorkshire. That season, at the age of twenty-three, he took 19 wickets for the Second XI.

His first-team debut in 1962 was one of only five appearances he made that summer, although his contribution for Hanging Heaton was far more significant – 82 wickets at 7.37 apiece. That return helped his club to win the Yorkshire Council Championship while he picked up the Council bowling award. His 66 wickets in Yorkshire's 1963 Championship winning season cost him just 16.87 runs apiece. By the time Yorkshire were next crowned County Champions, in 1966, Nicholson was an important member of the side.

A large, strong physique made him the ideal man to bowl into the wind, or as he referred to it 'up the cellar steps'. A whole-hearted, enthusiastic player, he bowled with an unusual action. A genuine swinger of the ball, his stock delivery was the out-swinger, but he could bowl an in-swinger, a good slower ball and a deceptive yorker. At a pace below fast-medium, his action enabled him to skid the ball through at times quicker than the batsman expected. Twice he took 100 wickets in a season; his best return was in 1966 when his 115 wickets cost only 15.50 each. Nicholson was close to being chosen for England on more than one occasion. He was selected for the 1964/65 tour of South Africa but injury prevented him from making the trip.

A modest batsman, his large build restricted his speed and mobility in the field and contributed to a lack of any international honours. Known as 'Teapot' by his team-mates, the name came from Nicholson's hands-on-hips pose as he glared at a batsman who, in his judgement, had just been plumb lbw. A jolly and immensely popular cricketer, a hard-earned benefit in 1973 earned him £13,214, before his eventual retirement. He coached and played at Markse after county cricket but was forced to give up his work as a brewery representative due to ill-health. A fine golfer, he was captain of Ripon City Golf Club at the time of his premature death. Nicholson gave great service to Yorkshire and played his part in five Championship-winning seasons in the 1960s. His wickets were most often obtained through honest hard work and bustling endeavour.

Chris Old

LHB and RFM, 1966-1982

Full Name: Christopher Middleton Old
Birth: Middlesbrough, 22/12/1948

Type of Player: Lower order left-hand batsman, right-arm fast medium bowler

First Class Career for Yorkshire:
Debut: v. Hampshire, Portsmouth, 1966
Matches: 222
Batting: 4,785 runs (Av. 23.22), 5 centuries.
Highest Score: 116 v. Indians, Park Avenue, Bradford, 1974
Bowling: 647 wkts (Av. 20.72), 5wi 24 times.
Best performance: 7-20 v. Gloucestershire, Middlesbrough, 1969
Fielding: 131 catches
Year of last match: 1982

Tests: 46, 1972/73-1981

Memorably described by Mike Brearley as being 'a displaced gene away from greatness', Chris Old was a quality seam bowler who had a lengthy Test career which produced 143 wickets. Old's talents at Acklam Hall Grammar School and Middlesbrough were such that he was equally good at batting and bowling. However, when he established his place in the county side it was as a replacement for Trueman. So quickly did he progress that he first played for England in 1970 in two unofficial 'Tests' against the Rest of the World. Injuries, a continuing feature of his career, delayed his full Test debut.

With a text-book action and a good height, Old made the ideal pace bowler. He could move the ball both ways off the seam and was able to use swing effectively when conditions allowed. He also played some important innings, the most famous being a significant 29 in support of Ian Botham at 'Headingley '81'. He had a good technique and his powerful hitting and driving were played straight, for example when he scored a century in 37 minutes against Warwickshire at Edgbaston in 1977. His fielding added another string to his bow and he was often to be found in the slips, even when playing for England.

Old was at his peak in the late 1970s, scoring a century and taking nine wickets in a Roses victory at Old Trafford in 1978. His best Test performance, 7-50, was against Pakistan at Edgbaston in the same year, helping his selection as one of the *Wisden* five. He was the only England player to appear in both Centenary Tests against Australia.

The granting of the county captaincy for the 1981 season placed Old in the firing line of Yorkshire's troubles and he was replaced by Illingworth during the following campaign. His reaction was to move to Warwickshire, and in 1984 he scored a half-century and took 11 for 99 at Headingley against the county of his birth.

It has been said that Old lacked a certain ruthlessness. He often bowled within himself and this proved effective in limited-overs cricket, his 306 wickets being a Yorkshire record. He took 1,070 wickets (average 23.48) in his first-class career and his 1979 benefit brought him £32,916. His best season was 1974 with 72 wickets at 18.97. He may not have fulfilled all the hopes that were expected of him but the memory of his fine bowling action and aggressive batting is very satisfying.

Edgar Oldroyd

RHB and RM/OB, 1910-1931

Full Name: Edgar Oldroyd
Birth: Healey, Batley, 01/10/1888
Death: Truro, Cornwall, 27/12/1964

Type of Player: Middle order right-hand batsman, right-arm medium pace/off-break bowler

First Class Career for Yorkshire:
Debut: v. Sussex, Anlaby Road, Hull, 1910
Matches: 383
Batting: 15,891 runs (Av. 35.23), 36 centuries. Highest Score: 194 v. Worcestershire, Worcester, 1923.
Bowling: 42 wkts (Av. 39.47). Best performance: 4-14 v. Gloucestershire, Anlaby Road, Hull, 1926.
Fielding: 203 catches
Year of last match: 1931

Tests: Nil

One of the best Yorkshire batsmen who never wore the England cap, Edgar Oldroyd made the number three position his own in the post-1918 era. This meant that he followed either Holmes or Sutcliffe to the crease and could have spent more time with his pads on, waiting to bat, than any other batsman in the history of the game. Bowlers were faced with a batsman who sold his wicket dearly. His technique was based on a sound defence and he was reliable and patient, to the point of being dour and dogged.

Oldroyd began as a medium-paced off-spinner for Stancliffe but a collection of seven shillings and sixpence for a half-century encouraged him to take batting more seriously. He found it difficult to establish himself in the county side, especially as the batting order varied so much and he often became too bogged down. By the time 1921 had arrived, however, he was a permanent fixture in the team.

He scored 1,000 runs for the first of ten consecutive seasons and 1922 remained his best with 1,690 runs at 43.33. He often scored important runs in low-scoring matches and became particularly renowned for his skill on difficult pitches. His courage against the sharply-rising ball was a feature of his steadfastness but he could also score fluently when conditions were in the batsman's favour. A 333-run stand with Holmes made against Warwickshire at Edgbaston in 1922 was the best of his ten double-century partnerships.

The most unfortunate event of Oldroyd's career came in the 1926 Roses battle at Old Trafford when he was knocked unconscious by a ball from Ted McDonald. Although he suffered no long-term effects, he was out for the rest of the season and the incident seemed to cloud the remainder of his career. His 1927 benefit brought him £1,700 and though he still produced the occasional valuable innings he seemed to lack some of his previous confidence against fast bowling. He became more security-conscious and was eventually not retained after the 1931 season, becoming professional with Pudsey St Lawrence.

Figures do not often do justice to a player's stature but it is worth noting that of the nineteen batsmen who have passed 15,000 runs for Yorkshire, only six have a better average than Oldroyd's. It seems extremely odd that he did not play in any type of representative fixture whatsoever. The selectors must not have wanted consistency and reliability.

Doug Padgett

RHB and RM, 1951-1971

Full Name: Douglas Ernest Vernon Padgett
Birth: Dirk Hill, Bradford, 20/07/1934

Type of Player: Opening/middle order right-hand batsman, right-arm medium pace bowler

First Class Career for Yorkshire:
Debut: v. Somerset, Taunton, 1951
Matches: 487
Batting: 20,306 runs (Av. 28.55), 29 centuries.
Highest Score: 161* v. Oxford University, The Parks, 1959
Bowling: 6 wkts (Av. 34.66). Best performance: 1-2 v. Derbyshire, Bramall Lane, Sheffield, 1964
Fielding: 250 catches
Year of last match: 1971

Tests: 2, 1960

On Yorkshire's pay-roll for almost fifty years, Doug Padgett was one of Yorkshire's most loyal employees and served it in periods of success and failure with an equally phlegmatic approach to all situations. At the age of thirteen Padgett was the youngest batsman to play in the Bradford League, for Idle, and was Yorkshire's then youngest-ever player when he made his debut at the age of 16 years and 321 days.

Described as the most technically and classically correct batsman of his era, he was neat, stylish and attractive. He passed 1,000 runs in 1956, for the first time, but was not given his county cap and even considered moving to Leicestershire. Three years later came Padgett's most famous innings. Yorkshire needed 215 runs in 105 minutes to defeat Sussex at Hove and win the Championship. That they did so with seven minutes to spare was almost entirely due to a third-wicket stand of 141 with Stott made in just over an hour, Padgett's contribution being a rapid but serene 79. This 1959 season remained his best summer with 2,181 runs (average 41.15) and he was rewarded with Test appearances in the following year.

An MCC tour to New Zealand, as part of a young side, followed. Although only Roger Prideaux exceeded Padgett's average and aggregate for the trip, he did not play in any of the representative matches and was never considered again.

An integral part of the Yorkshire side that won seven Championships, Padgett found himself with a new role when the team eventually broke up. At the end of the 1971 season, two years after his £7,385 benefit, he was appointed coach, a post which he fulfilled until the end of 1999, and second-team captain, remaining in this position for eight seasons. Padgett's main qualities for these roles were his own outstanding batting technique and the fact that he was a good judge of a player's abilities.

Ultimately, however, because of the county's failure to win anything other than two one-day trophies in the 1980s, his twenty-eight years attending to cricketing progress will be known as a period of intense disappointment, off-the-field troubles apart. He certainly had the respect of the players with whom he worked in a quiet and undemonstrative manner but the apparent lack of drive in making them into winners has told on his record.

Edmund Peate

LHB and SLA, 1879-1887

Full Name: Edmund Peate (registered Peat at birth)
Birth: Holbeck, Leeds, 02/03/1855
Death: Newlay, Horsforth, 11/03/1900

Type of Player: Tail end left-hand batsman, slow left-arm bowler

First Class Career for Yorkshire:
Debut: v. Nottinghamshire, Trent Bridge, 1879
Matches: 154
Batting: 1,793 runs (Av. 10.86). Highest Score: 95 v. Surrey, Dewsbury, 1884
Bowling: 794 wkts (Av. 12.57), 5wi 68 times. Best performance: 8-5 v. Surrey, Holbeck, 1883
Fielding: 97 catches
Year of last match: 1887

Tests: 9, 1881/82-1886

The first in Yorkshire's famous line of Test left-arm spinners, Edmund Peate was such a skilled practitioner that some who saw him and his two immediate successors, Peel and Rhodes, felt that he was the best. His end came under a cloud, though, as Hawke dispensed with the services of someone whose unruliness affected his performances and those of his team-mates.

Peate began his career as a quick bowler but realised, while playing for Manningham, that improved control of length and direction came with a slower pace. Some success at Scarborough led to promotion to the county XI and match figures of 12 for 77 came in only his third game, against Kent at Sheffield. He did not spin the ball to any great extent but relied instead on variation in flight, pace and length. His perfect action enabled the ball to turn almost naturally and this could be deadly on a helpful pitch.

In the summer of 1882 he bemused the Australians so much that he took 63 wickets (average 12.9) against them. With 214 wickets (average 11.52) in all matches, it remained his best season. Peate's part in the Oval Test of 1882 has been well documented and his phrase, 'I couldn't troost Maister Stood' referred to the fact that he felt that he must take the bowling, rather than a specialist batsman. Charles Studd, a Cambridge student, was playing in his first Test, and was clearly nervous. Peate's theory might have worked but he was out, England lost by seven runs, and has been villified ever since, despite that fact that he took eight wickets in the match.

His best Test performance, 6 for 85, was at Lord's two years later, also against Australia, and he finished his brief Test career with 31 wickets (average 22.00). Peate was a heavy drinker and this led to his downfall. He put on weight, his skill declined quickly and Hawke did the necessary, despite admitting later that it was one of his saddest tasks. It is to Peate's eternal credit that he bore Hawke no lifelong malice. 1,076 wickets (average 13.49) was his final first-class tally and he took two hat-tricks, both for Yorkshire.

For a few years, Peate was the best slow bowler in England, if not the world. He tormented the Australians at home and abroad and impressed many with his skill. That is how he should be remembered.

Bobby Peel

LHB and SLA, 1882-1897

Full Name: Robert Peel*
Birth: Churwell, Leeds, 12/02/1857
Death: Morley, 12/08/1941

Type of Player: Middle/lower order left-hand batsman, slow left-arm bowler

First Class Career for Yorkshire:
Debut: v. Surrey, Bramall Lane, Sheffield, 1882
Matches: 321
Batting: 9,378 runs (Av. 19.86), 6 centuries.
Highest Score: 210* v. Warwickshire, Edgbaston, 1896
Bowling: 1,334 wkts (Av. 15.70), 5wi 100 times.
Best performance: 9-22 v. Somerset, Headingley, 1895
Fielding: 141 catches
Year of last match: 1897

Tests: 20, 1884/85-1896

The successor to Ted Peate, Robert Peel was destined to become Yorkshire's second great slow left-arm bowler of the nineteenth century and, like his predecessor, contrived his own demise from first-class cricket. Peel's career overlapped Peate's by five years and in the main he played a supporting role until after 1887, when Peate departed.

Peel made an impressive start for Yorkshire, taking 9 for 129 on debut. He held his place in the team, despite being the second choice slow left-arm bowler, through the quality of his fielding (especially at cover-point) and as a forcing left-handed batsman. When Peate's career ended in unhappy circumstances, Peel really came to the fore.

A master of length, able to adapt his flight and pace according to the circumstances he encountered, Peel was quick to identify a batsman's weakness and exploit it. A shrewd and crafty exponent of his art, he had a quicker, almost medium-paced arm ball and on a helpful pitch was virtually unplayable. On good pitches he used meticulous accuracy and control to maintain supremacy, as his county captain Lord Hawke observed: 'No man ever took punishment as a bowler better, and it never made him shorten his length or send down a bad ball.'

The Lancashire and England captain A.C. MacLaren, who had in his own ranks Peel's great slow-left arm contemporary across the Pennines, Johnny Briggs, placed the Yorkshire wizard, 'first on my list of great left-handed bowlers on account of his wonderful judgement, his diabolical cleverness and his great natural ability.'

On 123 occasions he took five or more wickets in an innings and 33 times extended that to ten or more in the match. Eight times in first-class cricket he took 100 wickets in a season, his best return for Yorkshire (155 at 14.92 each) coming in 1895. He celebrated several noteworthy match performances in 1888, which brought *Wisden* recognition in 1889 – 12 for 62 against Lancashire; 14 for 33 at Sheffield against Nottinghamshire; and at Halifax, 13 for 84 versus Gloucestershire.

Some of his other special bowling efforts included 5 for 14 against Kent in 1887, 6 for 22 at Bristol in 1891 and 6 for 19 against Leicestershire at Scarborough in 1896. His one hat-trick for the county was taken at Halifax against Kent in 1897. Peel could bat too – over 12,000 runs serve to illustrate the point. The highest, and best of his six Yorkshire hundreds was scored at Edgbaston in 1896. He batted for nearly eleven hours for his 210 not out, adding 292 with Lord Hawke (166), still a county eighth-wicket record partnership. Combining his skills he achieved the double once in 1896, scoring 1,206 runs at 30.15 and taking 128 wickets at 17.50.

Australia were Peel's only Test opponents. He toured the country four times and by the close of his Test career he had become the first England bowler to take 100 wickets against them. More often than not when he encountered the Australians on a wet pitch, as he did several times, he was destructive. At Sydney in 1888, he and George Lohmann bowled them out for 42 and 82 on a 'sticky' track (Peel 9 for 58 in the match). Back in England a few months later, another rain-hit pitch at Manchester helped Peel (7 for 31 and 4 for 37) to continue the torment.

England's thrilling and dramatic ten-run victory at Sydney in December 1894, having had to follow on, seemed highly unlikely when Australia entered the final day needing only 64 more runs to win with eight second innings wickets intact. The previous evening, with the match all but lost, a number of the England players drank heavily to drown their sorrows, including Peel. The following morning a rain soaked pitch necessitated a sober Yorkshireman to help Briggs dismiss Blackham's Australians. When Peel finally realised that his side were back in with a chance he is reputed to have said to the captain: 'Give me the ball, Mr Stoddart, and I'll get t'boogers out before loonch!'. Good to his word, he (6 for 67) and Briggs (3 for 25) saw England to victory, two minutes before lunch. In his final Test at The Oval, his second innings, 6 for 23, saw Australia routed for 44.

The fall, when it came, was sad but perhaps not unexpected. A cheerful Victorian professional, Peel played hard and drank hard. When he took the field in 'a proper condition' at Bramall Lane on the final day of Yorkshire's fixture with Middlesex, Lord Hawke quickly banished him from sight. His dismissal from the county side followed. The suggestion that Peel urinated on the pitch during the incident at Sheffield was finally, and rightly, refuted and one hopes laid to rest by the eminent cricket historian Irving Rosenwater in 1997.

Slow left arm bowler Bobby Peel, a master of his art but victim of a self-induced fall from grace.

Returning to his roots, he played as Churwell's club professional after his shameful exit from county cricket, and with Accrington in the Lancashire League. Peel lived to the grand age of eighty-four and, despite his indiscretions, cricket has seen few greater slow-left arm bowlers than he.

George Pinder

RHB, SRA and WK, 1867-1880

Full Name: George Pinder* (real name George Pinder Hattersley)
Birth: Ecclesfield, Sheffield, 15/07/1841
Death: Hickleton, Doncaster, 15/01/1903

Type of Player: Lower order right-hand batsman, slow under-arm right-arm lob bowler, wicketkeeper

First Class Career for Yorkshire:
Debut: v. Surrey, The Oval, 1867
Matches: 124
Batting: 1,639 runs (Av. 10.64). Highest Score: 57 v. Gloucestershire, Clifton College, 1880
Bowling: 19 wkts (Av. 17.10). Best performance: 4-56 v. Surrey, The Oval, 1877
Wicket-keeping: 146 catches, 100 stumpings
Year of last match: 1880

Tests: Nil

A Yorkshire county captain in the 1870s, Joe Rowbotham described wicketkeeper George Pinder as 'the Dad of them all'. Although he only appeared in 124 matches for the county, he enhanced the reputation of White Rose 'keepers, established by Ned Stephenson. Thought of originally as a bowler, Pinder was a pocket-knife grinder by the age of ten. Having been brought up in the same street in Sheffield as the man he succeeded behind the stumps for Yorkshire (Stephenson), Pinder was keeping wicket for St Mary's CC by the age of eighteen.

By 1870, three years after his first appearance, he was the county's regular stumper and held off all rivals for a decade. His height (nearly six feet), long reach and sharp eye allowed him to take the fastest deliveries on either side of the wickets with style and a minimum of movement or fuss. Few 'keepers could have coped with the pace of 'Tear'em' Tarrant and John Jackson for All England, or Emmett, Freeman and Hill in the Yorkshire attack. Small wonder then that Pinder claimed to be the first to dispense with the customary position of long-stop.

The physical demands on the rough pitches of the day took a heavy toll on his poor hands, however. A.W. Pullin wrote in 1898: 'His finger joints are gnarled and distorted and he can move some of them in a way which nature's anatomy never intended they should be used.' A hard hitting lower order batsman, his best score for Yorkshire was 57, although his highest first-class innings (78) was for the North against South in 1873. A slow, under-arm lob bowler, he often kept his pads on while bowling.

He toured North America with Richard Daft's side in 1879 alongside his county team-mates Lockwood, Ulyett, Emmett and Bates. Awarded a benefit match in 1880 he received £300 from the match with Lascelles Hall. An invitation to join the Lord's staff was declined in the hope that his services were still required at Yorkshire. They were not, and Pinder fell on hard times until the formation of Hickleton Main Cricket Club in 1893, when he became their groundsman and storekeeper.

A proud, honest man who claimed he never gambled or appeared at a cricket match 'the worse for drink', Pinder's talent with the gloves was not forgotten and *Wisden* wrote after his death in 1903: 'To very fast bowling he was perhaps the best of all.'

Wilfred Rhodes

RHB and SLA, 1898-1930

Full Name: Wilfred Rhodes
Birth: Kirkheaton, 29/10/1877
Death: Branksome Park, Dorset, 08/07/1973

Type of Player: Right-hand batsman, slow left-arm bowler

First Class Career for Yorkshire:
Debut: v. MCC, Lord's, 1898
Matches: 883
Batting: 31,075 runs (Av. 30.08), 46 centuries.
Highest Score: 267* v. Leicestershire, Headingley, 1921
Bowling: 3,598 wkts (Av. 16.01), 5wi 252 times.
Best performance: 9-28 v. Essex, Leyton, 1899
Fielding: 586 catches
Year of last match: 1930

Tests: 58, 1899-1929/30

In terms of longevity of career, Wilfred Rhodes was Yorkshire's greatest cricketer. He is the only player to score over 30,000 runs and take over 3,000 wickets for the county and his final total of first-class wickets – 4,204 (average 16.72) – is a world record which may never be beaten. As with Hirst, Rhodes played firstly for Kirkheaton, but his path into the county side was by no means smooth.

His second club was Galashiels and he was awaiting a trial with Warwickshire when Peel was sacked, creating a vacancy for a place which was competed for with Albert Cordingley. Rhodes took 13 for 45 in his first Championship game against Somerset at Bath while Cordingley, sadly, attended his mother's funeral and that was that. So rapidly did Rhodes fit into the groove that 154 wickets (average 14.60) and second place in the national averages came in his first season. This brought him the honour of being one of *Wisden*'s Five Great Players of the Season and, as early as his third season, he created the Yorkshire record of 240 wickets in a campaign, his total of 261 (average 13.81) remaining a personal best.

He could spin the ball powerfully, and on better pitches deceived the batsman with flight and length, following his short run-up. It often appeared that he dropped each ball on the same tantalising spot, and even as fine a batsman as Victor Trumper once reputedly pleaded, 'Please, Wilfred, give me a little peace'. Although the brilliant Australian was on his way to 185, Rhodes conceded only 94 runs from his 48 overs at Sydney in 1903/04. Rhodes maintained to the end of his life that he was never hooked or cut. Meanwhile, a second string – batting – was being developed. Beginning at number eleven, Rhodes saw England through to a famous one-wicket victory, with Hirst, at The Oval in 1902 against Australia. Not content with that, he shared in a then record tenth-wicket stand of 130 with R.E. Foster against Australia at Sydney in 1903/04. Ten years after his debut he was opening for his country and remains the only England player to bat in all eleven positions in Test cricket.

Style was not his forte, but a sound technique and 'two or three effective strokes' (Sir Pelham Warner) were more than adequate in helping him to form the first

Wilfred Rhodes, demonstrating the bowling action that brought him a remarkable 4,204 first-class wickets.

great England pairing with Jack Hobbs. Rhodes, being such an intelligent cricketer, was an outstanding judge of a run and it was stated that the partnership had a perfect understanding when running together. Their best stand was 323 at Melbourne in 1911/12, Rhodes making his highest Test score of 179, and this remains England's record first-wicket partnership against Australia. It followed Rhodes' best season with the bat – 2,261 runs at 38.32.

During this period Yorkshire's younger bowlers came to the fore, but after 1918 Rhodes was needed again. Despite being well past the age of forty, he was as skillful as ever and topped the national averages four times in the first five seasons following the war. He was even recalled to the Test side in 1926, after a five-year gap, for a game at The Oval in which he made a significant contribution towards reclaiming the Ashes. Four years later his Test career concluded at the age of 52 years and 165 days having lasted for 31 years and 315 days; both of these remaining world records. His best innings figures were 8 for 68 in 1903/04, and the match figures of 15 for 124 remain the record for a Melbourne Test.

During an era of amateur captaincy, and particularly after the retirement of Hawke, Rhodes was effectively the county's leader on the field of play. With seven captains during the last sixteen seasons of Rhodes' career, there was plenty of opportunity to offer him the leadership but it was never taken – evidence of a misguided principle taken too far. At least he had the satisfaction of a testimonial in 1927, raising £1,821 to add to his £2,202 benefit of 1911.

The list of Rhodes' records is almost endless. His 1,110 first-class appearances are a world record, and 763 matches is a record for the Championship. He took 100 wickets in a season on a record 23 occasions and his total of 16 'doubles' is also unbeaten. After retirement he coached at Harrow School and retained a very keen interest in the game throughout his the rest of his long life. He continued to attend matches during his latter years and it was said that, despite being blind, he could understand exactly what was going on merely by listening to the sound of bat on ball.

Rhodes was an undemonstrative player, quiet, efficient and playing the game because it was his job of work, certainly not for fun. In this respect he was the opposite of Hirst, introvert and workmanlike; some would say even grim. His dourness typified the county's approach, particularly after the First World War. His outstanding success places him amongst the greatest of all cricketers and to describe him as the leading all-rounder in the world in the period from 1900 to 1939 would be no exaggeration.

Ellis Robinson

LHB and OB, 1934-1949

Full Name: Ellis Pembroke Robinson
Birth: Denaby Main, 10/08/1911
Death: Conisbrough, 10/11/1998

Type of Player: Lower order left-hand batsman, right-arm off-break bowler

First Class Career for Yorkshire:
Debut: v. Worcestershire, Worcester, 1934
Matches: 208
Batting: 2,597 runs (Av. 12.54). Highest Score: 75* v. Gloucestershire, County Ground, Bristol, 1937.
Bowling: 735 wkts (Av. 20.60), 5wi 43 times. Best performance: 8-35 v. Lancashire, Headingley, 1939
Fielding: 189 catches
Year of last match: 1949

Tests: Nil

I used to turn 'em too much', Ellis Robinson once knowingly declared and, with his long fingers, sturdy frame and good height, that was often the case. The amount of spin he imparted meant that he spent much of his career bowling round the wicket for Sellers' conquering Yorkshire side of the 1930s. A nephew of George Robinson, who played for Nottinghamshire in 1896, Ellis kept wicket as a boy in Denaby, South Yorkshire and arrived at Headingley bowling leg-breaks. Under advice from Hirst he was transformed into an off-spinner and although he was in the Yorkshire side of 1934, it took him until 1937 to be considered a 'regular'.

In 1938 he captured 104 wickets and in the last pre-war summer improved that tally to 120, including a hat-trick at Leeds against Kent and a career best (8 for 35) in the Roses match. His lower order batting was often called upon to supply quick runs and could hit the ball a long way when he was set. A brilliant close-to-the-wicket fielder, he won lasting fame alongside Mitchell, Yardley, Cyril Turner and skipper Sellers. At Bradford in 1938 he took six catches in Leicestershire's first innings (seven in the match); still a county record.

The Second World War, during which Robinson served six years in the RAF, robbed him of his prime years as a cricketer, but his best season was 1946 when his 167 first-class wickets (149 for Yorkshire) cost him only 14.95 each. He must have come close to playing for England but, despite a Test trial in 1946, he was not selected for Hammond's team to Australia that winter.

His county cap, testimonial of £1,500 and release by Yorkshire all came in 1949, but he was not finished with county cricket and spent three years plying his trade with Somerset. In his final season he claimed match figures of 15 for 78 at Weston-super-Mare against Sussex.

A loveable, honest and humble man, he frequently played under Brian Sellers' leadership, a man for whom he had the utmost respect. Yorkshire won five outright Championship crowns during Robinson's playing days. He was immensely proud of being made an honorary life member of the club in 1982. He lived close to Conisbrough Castle and in later life his passion was golf; indeed he was dressing for a round the day he passed away. A hard self critic, Robinson had no reason to doubt his contribution to Yorkshire's winning cause, be it with attacking late-order batting, superb close fielding or sharp spinning off-breaks.

Emmott Robinson

RHB and RFM, 1919-1931

Full Name: Emmott Robinson
Birth: Keighley, 16/11/1883
Death: Hinckley, Leicestershire, 17/11/1969

Type of Player: Middle order right-hand batsman, right-arm fast medium bowler

First Class Career for Yorkshire:
Debut: v. Warwickshire, Edgbaston, 1919
Matches: 413
Batting: 9,651 runs (Av. 25.53), 7 centuries.
Highest Score: 135* v. Leicestershire, Aylestone Road, Leicester, 1921
Bowling: 893 wkts (Av. 21.99), 5wi 36 times.
Best performance: 9-36 v. Lancashire, Park Avenue, Bradford, 1920
Fielding: 318 catches
Year of last match: 1931

Tests: Nil

Perhaps a greater character than a cricketer, Emmott Robinson personified Yorkshire cricket in the 1920s – uncompromising, serious, methodical and businesslike. Not chosen in the First XI until 1919, at the age of thirty-five, he gave his all to the county over the next dozen years or so. The apprenticeship was lengthy. Robinson played for the second team in 1906 and, despite performing with both bat and ball, was singularly overlooked before the First World War.

What you might term a 'bits and pieces' cricketer, Robinson was a medium-fast right-arm outswing bowler able to deliver a consistently good length. As a batsman he was cautious, determined to make the opposition work hard to earn his wicket – and even harder if the foe was Lancashire! – and he considered the cut shot too risky, almost sinful to play. Despite his age, he was agile and sharp in the field. D.C.F. Burton, Yorkshire captain from 1919 to 1921, remarked: 'On the offside Robinson's fielding was quite exceptional in its smartness.'

A serious man, Robinson simply could not play cricket 'for a laugh'. He hit 1,000 runs in a season twice for Yorkshire, with a best of 1,104 in 1921, and notched up seven first-class centuries. With the ball he passed the magical 100 wickets in a season once, in 1928. Amongst his bowling feats that year was 8 for 13 against Cambridge University, a side that Robinson, like a number of other pros, felt great bowling 'was wasted on'.

His heart and soul was Yorkshire cricket and its success and he applied all his cunning, experience and knowledge to that cause. Tales of Robinson's doings and sayings were largely captured by Neville Cardus who considered the craggy all-rounder 'as Yorkshire as Ilkley Moor or Pudsey'. Embellished or not, they serve as lasting examples of Robinson's passion for the game.

At Bradford in 1920, Robinson took his career best bowling figures of 9 for 36 when Lancashire, with six wickets in hand, needed only a further 52 for victory. Cardus, not having praised the Yorkshireman enough in his match report met with the retort: 'Ah suppose if Ah'd tekken all ten Lanky's wickets, tha'd have noticed me.'

Careful with his 'brass', a substantial benefit of £2,205 in 1930 helped swell the coffers and he later became a first-class umpire. His vast knowledge was put to good use as a coach at both Yorkshire and Leicestershire. Lean and wiry, he was Yorkshire's equivalent of grit and mettle.

Brian Sellers

RHB and OB, 1932-1948

Full Name: Arthur Brian Sellers, MBE
Birth: Keighley, 05/03/1907
Death: Eldwick, Bingley, 20/02/1981

Type of Player: Middle order right-hand batsman, right-arm off-break bowler

First Class Career for Yorkshire:
Debut: v. Oxford University, The Parks, 1932
Matches: 334
Batting: 8,949 runs (Av. 23.18), 4 centuries. Highest Score: 204 v. Cambridge University, Fenner's, 1936
Bowling: 8 wkts (Av. 81.62). Best performance: 2-10 v. Middlesex, Park Avenue, Bradford, 1933
Fielding: 264 catches
Year of last match: 1948

Tests: Nil

One of the greatest of all county captains, Brian Sellers will be remembered for his highly successful leadership in the 1930s but also for some misguided decisions which, with the benefit of hindsight, led to the county's least successful period in its entire history. Sellers led the first XI at St Peter's School, York, from the age of sixteen and gained further experience of leadership at Keighley in 1931. He led Yorkshire in his debut season, after Frank Greenwood's resignation, and from 1933 to 1947 in his own right, winning the County Championship six times in these nine seasons.

Although his father was chairman of the cricket committee at the time of his appointment, there is no doubting his credentials. Possessing all the qualities required of a successful leader, Sellers motivated those in his charge to achieve performances that made Yorkshire the outstanding team of the 1930s. He was a disciplinarian but also an outstanding tactician, understanding the opposition and how to use the prevailing conditions to best advantage. Never allowing any distractions to affect his leadership, in 1935 he lost the toss thirteen times and six players were used by England, but Yorkshire still won the title.

As far as his batting was concerned, he once began a season with four ducks, but he always compensated for his limited ability with sustained courage when facing fast bowlers and an ability to punish spinners. His best season was 1938, with 1,143 runs at 27.21, but a more significant effort came in 1946 when he finished third in the averages of a team which had been ravaged by the war effort but still managed to win the Championship yet again. Fielding was probably the most important aspect of Sellers' playing ability. He stood in suicidal positions and held some brilliant catches.

Selected as one of the *Wisden* five for 1940, Sellers was awarded the MBE for his part in the Second World War. He was Yorkshire's chairman from 1959 until 1972, overseeing another period of sustained success. However, he was directly responsible for the departures of Illingworth and Close and this will be held against him in some quarters. Despite the offence caused, it cannot be denied that Yorkshire's two most successful decades occurred while he held vital positions of responsibility.

Kevin Sharp

LHB and OB, 1976-1990

Full Name: Kevin Sharp
Birth: Leeds, 06/04/1959

Type of Player: Middle order left-hand batsman, right-arm off-break bowler

First Class Career for Yorkshire:
Debut: v. Northamptonshire, Scarborough, 1976
Matches: 195
Batting: 8,426 runs (Av. 29.56), 11 centuries. Highest Score: 181 v. Gloucestershire, Harrogate, 1976
Bowling: 12 wkts (Av. 69.66). Best performance: 2-13 v. Glamorgan, Park Avenue, Bradford, 1984
Fielding: 95 catches
Year of last match: 1990

Tests: Nil

One of the most attractive batsmen in Yorkshire's history, Kevin Sharp's story is one of ultimate disappointment as he failed to live up to high hopes. Two years younger than David Gower, with the same blond curls and left-handedness, his prolific run-scoring in youth cricket led to expectations of success developing along a similar career-path. Sharp played for Bingley and Leeds whilst still at Abbey Grange Church of England School but the vastness of his potential was first brought to the public's attention with his performances for England Under-19s. He scored a century against Australia in 1977 and in the following season, as captain, compiled 260 not out against West Indies at Worcester. *Wisden* described him batting 'so correctly and with so much skill' in an innings which was compiled in a total to which his team-mates could contribute only 99.

A first century for Yorkshire was made on Sharp's first visit to Lord's, for a game against Middlesex in 1980 but the first-class game, with its different challenges, proved a difficult task for him to tackle with any measure of consistency. It is probably fair to say that he only really enjoyed one season of success in his time on the county circuit. 1984 produced 1,445 runs (average 39.05) and that was the only campaign in which he passed 1,000. Illness, of a nervous type, dogged him in the early days and four full seasons was all that he could manage.

On his day he was a beautiful batsman to watch, with a wide range of attacking strokes, including some glorious ones on the off-side. Sharp scored 4,693 runs (average 29.00) in limited-overs matches for Yorkshire and played some important innings, occasionally as opener, in a type of cricket which often suited his aggressive style. The best of his three centuries was a knock of 114 against Essex at Chelmsford in the John Player League in 1985.

He was rewarded with a benefit of £89,770 in 1991 and captained Yorkshire's Second XI for one season before moving on to cricket development work in Shropshire. He returned to his native county in the autumn of 2000 to coach Leeds and Bradford Universities' Centre of Excellence. It was never easy for Sharp, in his playing career, and he never really gained a settled place. However, he maintained a cheerful disposition and gave considerable pleasure to those who watched him on his good days.

Phil Sharpe

RHB and OB, 1958-1974

Full Name: Philip John Sharpe
Birth: Shipley, 27/12/1936

Type of Player: Opening/middle order right-hand batsman, right-arm off-break bowler

First Class Career for Yorkshire:
Debut: v. Sussex, Worthing, 1958
Matches: 411
Batting: 17,685 runs (Av. 29.72), 23 centuries. Highest Score: 203* v. Cambridge University, Fenner's, 1960
Bowling: 2 wkts (Av. 70.00). Best performance: 1-1 v. Nottinghamshire, Headingley, 1968
Fielding: 525 catches
Year of last match: 1974

Tests: 12, 1963-1969

Amongst the best slip catchers of all time, Philip Sharpe was on a par with the likes of Frank Woolley, Wally Hammond, Bobby Simpson and his Yorkshire predecessor John Tunnicliffe. Born in Shipley, Sharpe went to Bradford Grammar School before moving, aged twelve, to Worksop College. There, from 1949 to1955, he played hockey, squash, tennis, rugby and cricket. He captained the school cricket XI in his final year and scored over 1,200 runs at an average of 113. In the holidays he played with Pudsey St Lawrence and, later, Bradford.

His first-class debut in 1956 was not for Yorkshire but Combined Services against Warwickshire. He had to wait another two seasons before his chance to represent the county arrived. A tendency to play 'chest on' in defence checked his early progress, but an unbeaten double century against Cambridge University and 152 against Kent in 1960 helped him to achieve 1,000 runs that season for the first time and his county cap. His ability in the field probably enabled him to keep his spot in the Yorkshire team at that time; it took him until 1962 to truly blossom as a batsman.

Relatively short (5 ft, 7 in.) and stocky, his cover-drive was first-rate and he enjoyed playing on hard, fast surfaces that allowed him to use the cut, pull and hook shots. He scored seven hundreds for Yorkshire in 1962, made 2,252 first-class runs and equalled Tunnicliffe's county record of 70 catches in a season. Chosen as the Young Cricketer of the Year, he was also amongst *Wisden*'s five in 1963. Perhaps lack of consistency at county level prevented Sharpe winning more than 12 Test caps. His England record shows he was comfortable at the highest level – 786 runs at an average of 46.23.

Many of his best Test knocks (including his four half centuries) came against the West Indians in 1963 and 1969. His one Test hundred was made at Trent Bridge against New Zealand. A fine baritone and music lover, Sharpe, usually with his great friend, team-mate Don Wilson, kept the Yorkshire dressing room entertained throughout the 1960s, and the two often travelled to games in Sharpe's MGB car. His benefit season raised £6,668 in 1971, and after his final season for Yorkshire he played a further two years with Derbyshire, nudging up his highest first-class score to 228, scored at The Parks in 1976. Sharpe's prowess at slip was down to several factors – stillness, concentration and an ability to delay the catch until the last second, when it appeared the ball had passed him by – those skills combined to make him not only one of the best close fielders of his era but one of the greatest ever.

Arnie Sidebottom

RHB and RFM, 1973-1991

Full Name: Arnold Sidebottom
Birth: Shawlands, Barnsley, 01/04/1954

Type of Player: Lower order right-hand batsman, right-arm fast medium bowler

First Class Career for Yorkshire:
Debut: v. Gloucestershire, Winget Ground, Gloucester, 1973
Matches: 216
Batting: 4,243 runs (Av. 22.33), 1 century.
Highest Score: 124 v. Glamorgan, Sophia Gardens, Cardiff, 1977
Bowling: 558 wkts (Av. 24.82), 5wi 22 times.
Best performance: 8-72 v. Leicestershire, Middlesbrough, 1986
Fielding: 60 catches
Year of last match: 1991

Tests: 1, 1985

One of the most durable of Yorkshire's pace bowlers, Arnie Sidebottom carried a weak attack through thick and thin, despite often being beset by injury. He always seemed to be nearly taking wickets. A bowler of considerable economy, especially in the limited-overs game, batsmen regularly played and missed to his off-cutters but he continued to bowl his heart out for the Yorkshire cause. Sidebottom played for ESCA at the age of fifteen, already having played for Barnsley.

He completed his schooling at Broadway School, also in Barnsley, and came into the Yorkshire side as an all-rounder, the county finding it difficult for several years to fit him into the side. However, it was his bowling that was needed most and so his batting tended to get neglected as the years progressed. He had a good technique and could bat anywhere in the order. In scoring his only century, he added 144 for the last wicket with Arthur Robinson.

Despite the demands that were placed on his vulnerable body, Sidebottom rarely flagged, always striving for wickets. His only Test match appearance was marred by injury, as he broke down as Ian Botham's opening partner at Trent Bridge against Australia. At least he had the satisfaction of taking a wicket first, even if it was the nightwatchman Bob Holland. Shins and feet were Sidebottom's recurring problem areas and he rarely completed a full season. When he did, he was able to produce as good a haul of wickets as 68 (average 23.38) in 1989.

The aggression of his early career had given way to bowling of a fuller length and he was very capable of exploiting any conditions that favoured swing or seam. Sidebottom took 258 wickets (average 26.52) in limited-overs matches, in addition to scoring over 1,000 runs. He was a very popular player, as evidenced by his 1988 benefit that produced a record £103,240.

Following retirement, he became coach at the Yorkshire Academy and for the 2000 season succeeded Padgett as senior coach on the county staff. This enabled him to work more closely with the first-team squad, including England players he had first assisted as schoolboys. For Sidebottom, the satisfaction that his new role brings is considerable. He toiled away as a bowler, now he encourages others to the kind of success that was just beyond his own abilities but which he fully deserved.

Chris Silverwood

RHB and RFM, 1993-present

Full Name: Christopher Eric Wilfred Silverwood
Birth: Pontefract, 05/03/1975

Type of Player: Lower order right-hand batsman, right-arm fast medium bowler

First Class Career for Yorkshire:
Debut: v. Hampshire, Southampton, 1993
Matches: 86
Batting: 1,431 runs (Av. 15.55). Highest Score: 58 v. Lancashire, Old Trafford, 1997
Bowling: 285 wkts (Av. 26.52), 5wi 14 times. Best performance: 7-93 v. Kent, Headingley, 1997
Fielding: 17 catches

Tests: 5, 1996/97-1999/2000

A key member of Yorkshire's rich crop of fast-medium bowlers to emerge in the late 1990s, Chris Silverwood, from Kippax, West Yorkshire, started out as a raw but talented YTS youngster at Headingley. Identified as a promising cricketer at Garforth Comprehensive, Silverwood was encouraged to attend net sessions in Pontefract where coach John Pearson nurtured him. After school came the YTS opportunity at Yorkshire and development at their Cricket Academy in Bradford.

Following his county debut, it took him three seasons to fulfil some of the obvious ability he had. He finished the summer of 1996 with 47 first-class wickets, including five wicket hauls against Worcestershire and Gloucestershire. Capped by Yorkshire that season, he was also the Cricket Writers' Young Cricketer of the Year and the only uncapped member of England's party to Zimbabwe and New Zealand that winter.

A promising Test debut against Zimbabwe at Bulawayo in December 1996 (4 for 71 in the match) didn't ultimately lead to an extended run in the England ranks. Called up from the 'A' side to join the senior party in the Caribbean on the 1997/98 tour as cover for the injured Darren Gough, he did not feature in the Test series. Injury to Dean Headley brought a call up, to England's tour of South Africa in 1999/2000. His second Test cap came at Port Elizabeth and he retained his position for the rest of the series. He claimed his first five wicket return (5 for 91) in the Fourth Test at Cape Town where England lost by an innings and 37 runs. He has played six one-day internationals for his country.

A committed pace bowler with a strong frame and long, bounding run-up, Silverwood's stamina was amply demonstrated against Kent at Headingley in 1997. With Yorkshire still in contention for the Championship title, he took a career best 7 for 93 in the visitor's first innings and 12 for 148 in the match from 51.3 overs. Despite this unstinting effort, Kent batted out for a draw and Yorkshire slipped to sixth position in the table. The leading Yorkshire bowler of 1999, with 59 wickets at 20.40 each, injuries in 2000 limited his involvement to 9 Championship outings and 26 wickets. Consolation for a frustrating season came with selection in England's 'A' West Indies tour in 2001.

A karate black belt who enjoys riding a motorbike, Chris Silverwood is only in his mid-twenties and a player of whom much is expected. He may yet justify the view of Australian batsman Justin Langer, who wrote in 1999: 'In terms of sheer pace, commitment and stamina, Chris Silverwood looks to be a young player destined to play more cricket for England.'

Frank Smailes

LHB and RM/OB, 1932-1948

Full Name: Thomas Francis Smailes
Birth: Ripley, Harrogate, 27/03/1910
Death: Starbeck, Harrogate, 01/12/1970

Type of Player: Lower order left-hand batsman, right-arm medium pace/off-break bowler

First Class Career for Yorkshire:
Debut: v. Oxford University, The Parks, 1932
Matches: 232
Batting: 5,686 runs (Av. 19.14), 3 centuries.
Highest Score: 117 v. Glamorgan, Cardiff Arms Park, 1938
Bowling: 802 wkts (Av. 20.68), 5wi 39 times.
Best performance: 10-47 v. Derbyshire, Bramall Lane, Sheffield, 1939
Fielding: 153 catches
Year of last match: 1948

Tests: 1, 1946

A model county cricketer and all-rounder, Frank Smailes was a pivotal member of Brian Sellers' side of the 1930s, always on hand to contribute with bat and ball when famous Yorkshire colleagues were absent on Test duty. Coached at cricket by his father and his elder brother, George, Smailes was a pupil at Pocklington Grammar School, where he learnt the basics of swing bowling. It took him three years to establish himself in the county first team as the obvious successor to George Macaulay.

A hard-hitting, attractive, left-handed runmaker, he was a safe, if not striking, fielder. Six feet tall, he had a high action, moved the ball late and, with a good command of length, bowled at a medium pace but could switch to bowling off-spin when conditions suited. Four times he took 100 or more wickets in a season. His best summer with the ball was 1936, when his 130 first-class wickets cost just 17.54 each. He disposed of seven Worcestershire batsmen in their second innings for only 24 runs at Headingley that season and took 10 for 62 in the match against the Indians.

His maiden first-class hundred was made against Warwickshire in 1937. Batting at number eight his century took just 100 minutes to compile. A year later the true measure of his all-rounder status was confirmed when he scored 1,002 runs and 113 wickets, amongst which were a number of exceptional performances. At Cardiff in June he hit a career best of 117 and 56 not out in the second innings and in the return fixture at Hull took 14 for 103 as the Welshmen were beaten by 12 runs.

He was also outstanding with the ball against the Australians at Bramall Lane, taking 6 for 92 and 4 for 45 which, but for rain, might have seen Bradman's side beaten. The weather also washed out the Third Test at Old Trafford when Smailes was selected in England's 13.

The advent of the Second World War plus the pre-war talent in England thwarted Smailes' chances of becoming a Test cricketer. He did make one appearance against India at Lord's in 1946, making 25 in his only innings and taking 3 for 62 in the match.

In his final season he was awarded a well earned benefit which realised £5,104. Before wartime service with the Royal Artillery, Smailes became only the third Yorkshireman to take all ten wickets in an innings. Figures of 10 for 47 (14 for 58 in the match) against Derbyshire at Bramall Lane in 1939 ensured him a permanent place in the county's bowling records.

Gerald Smithson

LHB and RM, 1946-1950

Full Name: Gerald Arthur Smithson
Birth: Spofforth, Harrogate, 01/11/1926
Death: Abingdon, Berkshire, 06/09/1970

Type of Player: Middle order left-hand batsman, right-arm medium pace bowler

First Class Career for Yorkshire:
Debut: v. Essex, Harrogate, 1946
Matches: 39
Batting: 1,449 runs (Av. 26.34), 2 centuries. Highest Score: 169 v. Leicestershire, Grace Road, Leicester, 1947
Bowling: 1 wkt (Av. 84.00). Best performance: 1-26 v. Nottinghamshire, Trent Bridge, 1947
Fielding: 21 catches
Year of last match: 1950

Tests: 2, 1947/48

A conscript 'Bevan Boy' – a National Serviceman who worked as a coal miner rather than in HM Forces – Smithson's selection for the 1947/48 MCC tour of the West Indies caused the matter to be raised in the House of Commons before the Government's permission to make the trip was finally secured. Born in Spofforth, near Harrogate, Smithson played his first cricket for Sidmouth, Devonshire, at the age of thirteen. His father, Harold, played professionally in the Bradford League and taught his son the art of groundsmanship, a skill which Smithson put to good use at Abingdon School after his county playing days. During his time as a Bevin Boy he played for the local colliery Askern.

The first of his 39 matches for Yorkshire was played in 1946. A forcing stroke player, his two hundreds for the county were both made in 1947. Forced to follow-on against Surrey at Bradford, Smithson batted four and a quarter hours in making an unbeaten and faultless 107 out of Yorkshire's 269 all out. Three weeks later he made 98 before lunch in his first Roses match. Yardley described that innings as 'one of the most polished displays of batting I have seen given by so young a player.' In the next match at Leicester he made his career highest score of 169, adding 196 for the second wicket with Len Hutton and 147 for the third wicket with Yardley.

He was one of five players capped by Yorkshire in 1947 and, along with Wardle, represented the county in the MCC party to tour the Caribbean. Finally cleared to make the trip, Smithson played in the first two Tests of the series. A duck on debut was followed by two scores of 35 in the drawn Second Test in Trinidad. An arm injury sustained in the West Indies forced him to miss the entire 1948 English season and he never recovered the form he had shown briefly for Yorkshire in 1947. Smithson made the move to Leicestershire in 1951, and in his second season there passed 1,000 runs (1,351 at an average of 27.57) in a season for the only time in his first-class career.

After leaving Grace Road in 1956 he coached in Surrey, before his long association at Abingdon in Berkshire. He played regularly for Hertfordshire from 1957 to 1962. An attractive batsman and good outfielder, Smithson's gifted potential, briefly glimpsed by Yorkshire in 1947, never fully materialised. The Bevan Boy is remembered more for the debate his England selection caused than the talent that originally won him the honour.

Ned Stephenson

RHB, RF and WK, 1861-1873

Full Name: Edwin Stephenson (known as Ned)
Birth: Sheffield, 05/06/1832
Death: Liverpool, 05/07/1898

Type of Player: Middle order right-hand batsman, right-arm fast round-arm bowler, wicketkeeper

First Class Career for Yorkshire:
Debut: v. Surrey, The Oval, 1861
Matches: 42
Batting: 878 runs (Av. 12.91). Highest Score: 67 v. Surrey, The Oval, 1863
Bowling: n/a
Wicket-keeping: 35 catches, 28 stumpings
Year of last match: 1873

Tests: Nil

Known as Edward or more commonly Ned, Stephenson was a serious faced, droll character from Sheffield and was Yorkshire's first wicketkeeper following the Club's official formation in 1863. He was, however, much more than just a stumper; a good batsman, he also bowled fast round-arm.

His first engagement as a cricketer, at the age of seventeen, was with J.W.R. Wilson at Broomhead Hall in Sheffield from 1849 to 1851. He went to four different clubs as professional in successive seasons and was serving at Christ Church, Oxford in 1857 when he accepted a job as a bowling professional with the MCC at Lord's. Although never selected to appear for the Players against the Gentlemen, Stephenson's breakthrough came in 1856 when he made his debut for both the All England XI and the United All England XI, having had success against them in local cricket.

A solid batsman with a good defence based around a long forward reach, he was capable, with his sturdy frame, of hard, punishing play. His batting, though, had a tendency towards circumspection which encouraged derision from the paying public. In Yorkshire's first match after their 1863 birth, Stephenson proudly top-scored with 67 against Surrey and hit the highest score (54) in the first-ever Roses encounter at Whalley in 1867.

The honour of making England's first run on Australian soil was also his when the historic 1861/62 tour got underway. A whimsical soul, Stephenson 'was always saying something to put a roomful into a roar of laughter' wrote William Caffyn, who toured with him to Australia. On the ship home from that first trip, the merry Yorkshire 'keeper remarked that the Red Sea didn't seem any redder than any other he had seen. A practical joker, he was often on the receiving end, such as the time he travelled six miles for a single-wicket challenge with one John Buggins, only to discover upon arrival that it was nothing more than a prank.

In 1870 he became the first Yorkshire player to be awarded a benefit match. The game took place at Bramall Lane, although Stephenson didn't take part. The United North beat the United South in two days. His decline into 'poor circumstances' was probably self-inflicted, a fondness for drink hastening the fall. He could usually be found in the Plough Inn at Hallam, and later lived in Liverpool. Stephenson has been long since forgotten as one of Yorkshire's 'best all-round cricketers of his time.'

Graham Stevenson

RHB and RMF, 1973-1986

Full Name: Graham Barry Stevenson
Birth: Ackworth, 16/12/1955

Type of Player: Lower order right-hand batsman, right-arm medium fast bowler

First Class Career for Yorkshire:
Debut: v. Middlesex, Park Avenue, Bradford, 1973
Matches: 177
Batting: 3,856 runs (Av. 20.84), 2 centuries. Highest Score: 115* v. Warwickshire, Edgbaston, 1982
Bowling: 464 wkts (Av. 28.56), 5wi 17 times. Best performance: 8-57 v. Northamptonshire, Headingley, 1980
Fielding: 73 catches
Year of last match: 1986

Tests: 2, 1979/80-1980/81

One of the most unfulfilled all-round talents of recent Yorkshire cricket, Graham Stevenson was an uncomplicated cricketer, capable of match-winning performances with bat and ball. The prodigious talent was evident in Stevenson's play aged fourteen, when he scored a century for Ackworth second team. He attended Minsthorpe High School, South Elmsall, and played with the Yorkshire Schools Cricket Association before joining Barnsley in 1972.

He played his first match for the county at the age of seventeen and his first two wickets were those of Middlesex and England's Mike Brearley and Clive Radley. Boycott played an influential part in Stevenson's early development, offering encouragement and technical help with his game and arranging a pre-season net for the youngster at Yorkshire.

A powerfully-built man, he was a fierce hitter of the cricket ball. The second of his two first-class centuries was made batting at number eleven in the order. He and Boycott (79) added 149 for the tenth wicket against Warwickshire in 1982 – still a county record partnership for the last wicket. A good one-day cricketer, he took 290 wickets for Yorkshire and scored 1,699 runs, including a stunning 81 not out in the Somerset Sunday League game in 1984, made from just 29 balls faced with 10 sixes.

A busy, orthodox, fast-medium right-arm bowler, he lacked consistency even before a number of injuries forced a reduction in pace. In the right conditions though he caused damage. He took 8 for 65 in the Roses match at Leeds in 1978 (the year he won his county cap) and his 7 for 48 at Trent Bridge two years later included a spell of 5 for 0. On a rain-affected pitch at Abbeydale in 1979 he dismissed six Warwickshire batsmen for 14 runs.

He played twice for England in Tests (28 runs and 5 wickets). He made 27 not out in Bombay against India in 1980 in a match dominated by Ian Botham and his best effort with the ball was 3 for 111 against West Indies in Antigua, 1981. He appeared in four one-day internationals and his most glorious moment was during the day/night match at Sydney on the 1979/80 tour of Australia when, needing 35 to win, with only two wickets standing and 30 balls left, he struck a quick-fire 28 not out to see England home.

A move to Northamptonshire in 1987 did not work out and he left county cricket behind without even a benefit to reward his mercurial abilities. The characteristics Stevenson lacked that could have made him a 'complete all-rounder' were a 'Boycott-like' determination and application, together with a greater self belief in his own gifts as a cricketer.

Bryan Stott

LHB and RM, 1952-1963

Full Name: William Bryan Stott
Birth: Yeadon, 18/07/1934

Type of Player: Opening left-hand batsman, right-arm medium pace bowler

First Class Career for Yorkshire:
Debut: v. Scotland, Hamilton Crescent, Glasgow, 1952
Matches: 187
Batting: 9,168 runs (Av. 31.61), 17 centuries. Highest Score: 186 v. Warwickshire, Edgbaston, 1960
Bowling: 7 wkts (Av. 16.00). Best performance: 4-34 v. Surrey, The Oval, 1962
Fielding: 89 catches
Year of last match: 1963

Tests: Nil

Between 1957 and 1963, Bryan Stott formed a fast-scoring opening partnership with Ken Taylor that gave the Yorkshire teams of the day a firm but brisk base on which to build. A stocky, hard hitting top order batsman, he first played the game at Aireborough Grammar School from where Brian Close had previously emerged. He played for both the Yorkshire and England Schoolboy sides and topped the Yorkshire Second XI batting averages in 1951. He was called upon to perform as twelfth man during the Leeds Test match with South Africa having just reached the age of seventeen. A year later he made his first appearance for Yorkshire but it wasn't until 1957, when he was capped, that he firmly established a regular place in the side.

Stott had five really good seasons for Yorkshire, with the Championship year of 1959 standing out. Although he scored 1,000 runs in a season on five occasions, topping the county averages in 1958 and 1960, 1959 was his best summer in terms of runs scored – 2,034 at an average of 37.66. He carried his bat for 144 not out at Worcester and scored 96 at Hove as Yorkshire successfully chased 215 runs to win in 105 minutes and claim an unlikely Championship title. He batted for only 86 minutes, scored 13 of the 15 runs that came in the first over of the second innings and added 141 for the third wicket with Padgett in just over an hour. Together he and Taylor raised three double-century opening partnerships, the highest of which was an unbroken 281 against Sussex at Hove in 1960. An absolute confidence and understanding existed between the pair, and their running between the wickets was exceptional. The highest of his first-class hundreds took six and a quarter hours to compile, and his seventeenth and final century (143) was made at Sheffield against Lancashire in June 1963.

He announced his retirement that season to concentrate on the family business and spent six good years playing cricket at Harrogate. A Yorkshire committee member from 1982 until 1993, he was closely involved with the work that led to the establishment of the Cricket School and the Academy. Stott was only twenty-nine when he left Yorkshire to attend to his business affairs. Life away from cricket no doubt helped him to appreciate how lucky he had been to play the game for a living and to have contributed as he did to four Yorkshire Championship triumphs.

Herbert Sutcliffe

RHB and RM, 1919-1945

Full Name: Herbert Sutcliffe
Birth: Summerbridge, Pateley Bridge, 24/11/1894
Death: Cross Hills, Keighley, 22/01/1978

Type of Player: Opening right-hand batsman, right-arm medium pace bowler

First Class Career for Yorkshire:
Debut: v. Gloucestershire, Spa Ground, Gloucester, 1919
Matches: 602
Batting: 38,558 runs (Av. 50.20), 112 centuries. Highest Score: 313 v. Essex, Leyton, 1932
Bowling: 8 wkts (Av. 47.62). Best performance: 2-16 v. Surrey, The Oval, 1937
Fielding: 401 catches
Year of last match: 1945

Tests: 54, 1924-1935

One of the greatest batsmen of all time, Herbert Sutcliffe concluded his Test career with an average – 60.73 – which has never been improved upon by any Englishman. He was most fortunate in having partnerships that produced, with Jack Hobbs, the best-ever Test pairing, and, in Holmes, an alliance whose output has never been surpassed in first-class cricket. Sutcliffe moved to Pudsey as a baby. He played for both of the town's clubs, as well as others, including West of Scotland, before settling into the county side.

He made an immediate impact, scoring five centuries, topping the Yorkshire averages and finding himself one of the *Wisden* Five in the 1920 edition. 1922 was the first season that established him as a player of real quality. He scored the first of his 16 double centuries, passed 2,000 runs for the first of 14 consecutive seasons (an unbeaten record) and, most significantly, opened the batting for the first time with Hobbs – for the Players at Scarborough. Further successes in 1923 ensured that he made his Test debut in the following season, and the new pair produced a stand of 268 together in their second game against South Africa, breaking the record for a Test in England. He was able to develop a similar understanding with Hobbs as he had with Holmes with regard to running between the wickets. He was the junior partner to both, learnt to have complete confidence and trust and could not distinguish between them in this facet of the game. Their running was described on one occasion as being 'daring to the point of audacity'.

More Test records fell Sutcliffe's way in Australia in 1924/25. He became the first English player to score two centuries in the same match and he and Hobbs became the first pair from any country to bat through a full day's play. Sutcliffe completed 1,000 runs in his first ten matches and he remains the only English batsman to achieve this feat. An impeccable technique and an imperturbable temperament were the basis of Sutcliffe's play. The more difficult the pitch to bat on, the greater his powers of concentration. Nowhere was this more evident than in the final Test of 1926. A seven-hour innings of 161, following an overnight thunderstorm, laid the foundations of a score of 434 and the subsequent regaining of the Ashes amid

Herbert Sutcliffe walks out to open the innings for England with Jack Hobbs (wearing a cap). Together the famed opening pair shared fifteen century stands for their country.

jubilant scenes at The Oval.

The obduracy of his batting, however, was only so when the occasion necessitated it. He had an outstanding judgement of length, pace and direction and, despite an alleged lack of classical strokes, could score very rapidly, being a strong player off either foot. While touring South Africa in 1927/28, Sutcliffe received a cable from the county committee offering him the Yorkshire captaincy, providing that he became an amateur. However, the sting in the tail was that a players' poll showed that they preferred Rhodes and the invitation was withdrawn. Sutcliffe conceded gracefully and the post went to William Worsley, who had never even played first-class cricket!

The period 1928-32 showed Sutcliffe at his peak. He scored 3,000 runs in three of these five seasons and topped the national averages for each of the last three. 1929 was his benefit season, producing £3,056, but in the following year his Test partnership with Hobbs ended. Their record of 11 opening century stands against Australia may remain forever, as could their average stand of 87.81 against all countries.

In 1931 Sutcliffe achieved his best average (96.96) and took part in two triple century stands with Holmes. These merely whetted the appetite for their record-breaking 555 in the following season, when Sutcliffe scored his only triple-century. He made his 100th century with 132 against Gloucestershire and finished his best season with 3,336 runs at 74.13. His highest Test score, 194 at Sydney, came in the following winter's infamous 'bodyline series' but the Australians' respect for his batting was tainted by their criticism of his support for Jardine's tactics. However, he ended his career against Australia with an average of 66.85 – an outstanding record which still remains.

The end of the 1933 season saw an end to the most prolific of all partnerships, when Holmes was not re-engaged. A new generation was beginning, however, and Sutcliffe shared nine century-opening stands with Hutton in 1937. There was no real waning of his powers, and in 1939 he became the oldest player to carry his bat through a first-class innings. Sutcliffe's career ended with 50,670 runs (average 52.02), including 151 centuries. He was a Test selector for three seasons from 1959 and has a permanent memorial at Headingley in the shape of the 'Sutcliffe Gates', erected in 1965. The inscription, 'In Honour of a great Yorkshire and England cricketer', has never had a truer ring.

Ken Taylor

RHB and RM/LB, 1953-1968

Full Name: Kenneth Taylor
Birth: Primrose Hill, Huddersfield, 21/08/1935

Type of Player: Opening/middle order right-hand batsman, right-arm medium pace/leg break bowler

First Class Career for Yorkshire:
Debut: v. Northamptonshire, Headingley, 1953
Matches: 303
Batting: 12,864 runs (Av. 27.37), 16 centuries.
Highest Score: 203* v. Warwickshire, Edgbaston, 1961.
Bowling: 129 wkts (Av. 28.52), 5wi once.
Best performance: 6-75 v. Lancashire, Old Trafford, 1961
Fielding: 146 catches
Year of last match: 1968

Tests: 3, 1959-1964

Ken Taylor was one of Yorkshire's greatest cover-point fielders and a gifted sportsman. Born in Huddersfield, he attended Stile Common School and, with a talent for art, later studied at Slade School of Fine Arts in London. Like his younger brother, Jeff, he was a good soccer player and was able to combine a professional career in both football and cricket. A regular member of the Yorkshire second team by the age of fifteen, he played for Huddersfield Boys, Yorkshire Boys and English Schools at cricket. A good centre-half, he made over 300 Football League appearances for Huddersfield Town and Bradford City between 1953 and 1966.

His first full Yorkshire appearance at cricket came in 1953, although it took him three seasons to establish himself. Capped in 1957, having produced 'several fine displays' that year, it was not until 1959 that his dashing opening batting brought him 1,000 runs in a season for the first time. He passed that particular landmark on five other occasions, recording his best aggregate in 1961 when he scored 1,494 runs at 34.74 per innings. His only double hundred was also made that season. He batted for almost five and a half hours in recording his career-best score and hit 1 six and 28 fours.

A good straight driver of the ball, he played the late cut particularly well and habitually stole quick singles. Medium in pace, his accurate seam bowling yielded 129 victims for Yorkshire and this allied with his quality in the field made him worthy of all-rounder status. Taylor won three Test caps for England, two against India in 1959 and one against Australia at Leeds five years later, but without any success. His top score was a modest 24 on his debut at Trent Bridge. Yorkshire lost the services of Illingworth, Trueman and Taylor after 1968, the latter two to retirement.

Granted a benefit in his final year, Taylor received the sum of £6,301. He has coached cricket in South Africa and New Zealand and played for Norfolk between 1972 and 1974. Art master at Gresham's School, his artistic skills have been adapted to cricketing portraits in recent times and Taylor's work has been captured and used in two nostalgic books on county cricket in the 1950s and 1960s by author Stephen Chalke. An individual blessed with many skills, Yorkshire County Cricket Club were fortunate to share in Taylor's sporting prowess.

John Thewlis

RHB and RM, 1862-1875

Full Name: John Thewlis*
Birth: Kirkheaton, 30/06/1828
Death: Lascelles Hall, 29/12/1899

Type of Player: Opening right-hand batsman, right-arm medium pace round-arm bowler

First Class Career for Yorkshire:
Debut: v. Surrey, Bramall Lane, Sheffield, 1862
Matches: 47
Batting: 1,317 runs (Av. 15.86), 1 century.
Highest Score: 108 v. Surrey, The Oval, 1868
Bowling: n/a
Fielding: 25 catches, 1 stumping
Year of last match: 1875

Tests: Nil

The most celebrated member of the cricketing brotherhood of Lascelles Hall, John Thewlis, like Hirst and Rhodes, was born in Kirkheaton. He lived a life of 'courage born of poverty'. He taught himself to read and write and play cricket, having never attended school for fear of ridicule about his natural white hair. Although he was thirty-four when Yorkshire CCC was formed in 1863, he was the only player not to miss a match for the county in their first three seasons and, against Surrey in 1868, he scored the Club's first ever century. *Scores and Biographies* described Thewlis as 'a good steady batsman' and also 'an excellent long stop'. He played cricket for Lascelles Hall and followed his occupation there as a fancy weaver.

Recommended to George Parr, captain of the All England XI, by his great friend Luke Greenwood, Thewlis finally played his first 'important' match in 1862 against the United All England XI at Lord's. Opening the batting, he made scores of just 5 and 4. The same season in which he became Yorkshire's first centurion, Thewlis appeared at the age of forty in the Players against Gentlemen fixture, the confirmation of a cricketer's high rank. The Thewlis family connections were rich and deep and the introduction of Ephraim Lockwood to the Yorkshire side was credited to his Uncle John's recommendation.

In his last season of 'big time' cricket, in 1875, a benefit game was played for the Lascelles Hall veteran at Sheffield, Yorkshire playing Gloucestershire. He took with him a sum of around £350 into a long and obscure retirement. 'John Thewlis is not dead. He is living at No.782, Oldham Road, Failsworth, near Manchester' wrote A.W. Pullin in the winter of 1898, having uncovered the forgotten old Yorkshire player carrying a basket of heavy laundry for four miles into Manchester to earn a few coppers. The article, which appeared as one of a series of features on old cricketers in the *Yorkshire Evening Post*, stirred the county into giving Thewlis a winter allowance and old friends found him a job as groundsman to the Greenfield Club for the summer.

The escape from relative poverty was brief, however. Returning home to Lascelles Hall for Christmas in 1899, he was taken ill and he died in late December. 'Tow' Thewlis should not have been allowed to sink into such hardship and oblivion; Yorkshire's first centurion deserved much better.

Fred Trueman

RHB and RF, 1949-1968

Full Name: Frederick Sewards Trueman, OBE
Birth: Stainton, Maltby, 06/02/1931

Type of Player: Lower order right-hand batsman, right-arm fast bowler

First Class Career for Yorkshire:
Debut: v. Cambridge University, Fenner's, 1949
Matches: 459
Batting: 6,852 runs (Av. 15.15), 2 centuries.
Highest Score: 104 v. Northamptonshire, Northampton, 1963
Bowling: 1,745 wkts (Av. 17.12), 5wi 97 times.
Best performance: 8-28 v. Kent, Dover, 1954
Fielding: 325 catches
Year of last match: 1968

Tests: 67, 1952-1965

The enduring memories of those who witnessed 'Fiery' Fred Trueman in his pomp must surely be the rolling up of the flapping shirt sleeve in the walk back to his mark; the tossing back of the wayward locks of black hair before the smooth accelerated run to the wicket culminating with a high cartwheel action and drag of the back foot through the crease. Unquestionably Yorkshire's greatest fast bowler and the first in the history of Test cricket to take 300 wickets, Trueman is one of English cricket's icons. The miner's lad left school in Maltby, Rotherham at the age of fourteen to start his working life in a factory. Encouraged by his father to play cricket, he bowled quickly at school and with local side Roche Abbey CC before a move in 1948 to Sheffield United.

In those early days he was rapid, but also wayward and liable to be punished accordingly. He hadn't appeared for the Colts when his first team chance came in 1949. He also played in the next fixture against Oxford University and took match figures of 6 for 72 in Yorkshire's 69-run defeat. He made his first notable contribution a month later with second innings figures of 8 for 70 at Lord's against the Minor Counties. An injury in the match against the Kiwis at Sheffield in late July ended Trueman's first eventful summer.

Away from cricket, he worked at the local colliery but often did the night shift in order to play in a big game. In 1951 he established a regular spot in the county side and, although overshadowed by Appleyard's achievement of 200 wickets, Trueman's 90 wickets at 20.57 apiece was pleasing progress. He captured the first of four career hat-tricks (all for Yorkshire – a county record with Macaulay) against Nottinghamshire that season in the course of first innings figures of 8 for 53. In the home fixture at Sheffield against the same county the preceding month he had bowled 'at very fast pace and frequently made the ball fly' recorded *Wisden*, to claim 8 for 68.

National Service claimed Trueman in 1952, although the RAF were charitable in the demands they placed on the young fast bowler, allowing him to continue his development in the game. That year also witnessed a stunning Test debut at Headingley. Opening the bowling with Alec Bedser, Trueman (3 wickets in 8 balls) reduced India's second innings to nought for 4 in one of the most legendary spells from the Kirkstall Lane End. His best Test figures (8 for 31) also came during that first series in the Third Test at Old Trafford. Perhaps at his quickest that summer, he was twenty-one years of age, stood

Fred Trueman is applauded off the field by his England team mates at The Oval in 1964, after becoming the first bowler to take 300 Test wickets. Also pictured, from left to right: Ted Dexter, John Price, Colin Cowdrey, Jim Parks, Ken Barrington, Tom Cartwright, Jack Crapp (umpire), Peter Parfitt.

5 ft 10 in. and weighted in at around 13 1/2 stones – a fearsome proposition for any batsman.

The impact was immediate: Trueman was the Cricket Writer's Club choice as Young Cricketer of the Year and selection in *Wisden*'s five soon followed. Trueman made the last of his 67 Test appearances in 1965 and although he toured both West Indies and Australia twice, he was not selected for the MCC sides of Australia (1954/55) or South Africa (1956/57). A forthright, outspoken player, his comments did cause a clash with authority and certainly played a part in him not winning more Test caps.

Despite those difficulties, at 2.45 p.m. on Saturday, 15 August 1964, Neil Hawke of Australia edged a catch to Colin Cowdrey and Fred Trueman had become the first bowler to take 300 Test wickets. His final haul, 307 Test wickets, cost him only 21.57 runs each and he remained the leading Test wicket-taker until 1975/76 and the England record holder until passed by Bob Willis in 1983/84.

As the belligerence and raw pace of youth faded over the years, so in its place came a complete mastery of the bowling arts. Trueman varied his line of attack with great shrewdness, using the yorker and the bouncer to keep the batsman thinking, and the slightest hint of uncertainty brought a shorter, quicker delivery. Strength, determination and stamina were amongst his greatest attributes, and with maturity came a control of seam and swing. He took 100 wickets in a season on 12 occasions, with a best return of 175 wickets in 1960 at only 13.98.

A batsman who liked to entertain, Trueman combined a good defence with a range of bold, attacking strokes. Three first-class centuries served to prove that he was a more than capable hitter. Fielding close in, often on the leg side, he was a fine catcher and when he deputised as Yorkshire's skipper he proved to be a shrewd and intelligent exponent of the craft. The county's victory over the Australians in 1968 illustrated the judgement.

A journalist, TV personality and a highly respected broadcaster and commentator after his playing days, Trueman was awarded a long overdue OBE in 1989. As with all 'characters', many of the stories told about him over the years have been embellished, but beyond question he breathed life and humour into any cricket match. The last word, though, must go to his biographer and great friend, the late John Arlott, who wrote: 'For a decade – again much longer than the peak period of even the best of the kind – he was, when the fire burned, as fine a fast bowler as any.'

John Tunnicliffe

RHB and SRA, 1891-1907

Full Name: John Tunnicliffe*
Birth: Low Town, Pudsey, 26/08/1866
Death: Westbury Park, Bristol, 11/07/1948

Type of Player: Opening right-hand batsman, slow right-arm bowler

First Class Career for Yorkshire:
Debut: v. Nottinghamshire, Trent Bridge, 1891
Matches: 475
Batting: 19,477 runs (Av. 27.20), 22 centuries. Highest Score: 243 v. Derbyshire, Chesterfield, 1898
Bowling: 7 wkts (Av. 55.28). Best performance: 1-6 v. Hampshire, Park Avenue, Bradford, 1899
Fielding: 667 catches
Year of last match: 1907

Tests: Nil

Long John' Tunnicliffe was probably the best Yorkshire player never to appear for England. An opening batsman of considerable success, he was also a very fine slip fielder. He was tall and had long arms, but he also knew instinctively where to stand for each bowler, whatever the conditions. The first in the famous line of Pudsey-reared cricketers, Tunnicliffe played for the Britannia club from the age of sixteen.

Although he made his debut for the county second XI two years later, he waited for his first-class debut for a further seven years, possibly because of his spectacular style of hitting. He discovered that he would need to tighten his defence in order to succeed at the higher level and it was not until 1895 that he scored a century or passed 1,000 runs in a season for the first time. He had to abandon many of his freer hits but retained their power, even clearing the pavilion at Bramall Lane.

Once he had gained a settled place in the side, Tunnicliffe continued to play in a solid manner and formed an outstanding opening partnership with Brown. Their record of 19 century stands has been beaten by only four Yorkshire pairs and when Tunnicliffe made his highest score, the duo set a world record for the highest stand for any wicket. This mammoth partnership of 554 stood as a record for 34 years, to be beaten by Holmes and Sutcliffe.

In 1901 Tunnicliffe took 70 catches, a record which stood for 27 years, and was elected as one of the *Wisden* five. Two years later he received £1,750 for his benefit. Tunnicliffe took an average of 1.41 catches per match and this is easily the best for the county. The speed of his reflexes overcame any disadvantage brought about by his height and he was able to dive considerable distances. He twice took seven catches in a match – a record equalled by only three other players in the history of the game.

There was no waning of his powers with increased age but, having scored 1,195 runs in the 1907 season, he retired. He took a coaching post at Clifton College, as well as with Gloucestershire, later serving on the committee of that county. Tunnicliffe will not be remembered as a colourful player, but his dependable batting and spectacular fielding should have brought him greater rewards.

George Ulyett

RHB and RF, 1873-1893

Full Name: George Ulyett*
Birth: Crabtree, Pitsmoor, Sheffield, 21/10/1851
Death: Pitsmoor, Sheffield, 18/06/1898

Type of Player: Opening right-hand batsman, right-arm fast bowler

First Class Career for Yorkshire:
Debut: v. Sussex, Bramall Lane, Sheffield, 1873
Matches: 359
Batting: 14,351 runs (Av. 24.20), 15 centuries.
Highest Score: 199* v Derbyshire, Bramall Lane, Sheffield, 1887
Bowling: 460 wkts (Av. 17.88), 5wi 21 times.
Best performance: 7-30 v. Surrey, Bramall Lane, Sheffield, 1878
Fielding: 238 catches
Year of last match: 1893

Tests: 25, 1876/77-1890

Universally known as 'Happy Jack', Ulyett was considered by no less a judge than W.G. Grace to be 'unquestionably the greatest all-round cricketer Yorkshire ever produced.' The burly, big-hearted Sheffield sportsman had a jovial and enthusiastic approach to life and cricket and conveyed that to colleagues and opponents throughout his 20 years of service with the county.

Ulyett followed his brother Jack into the Pitsmoor cricket team at the age of sixteen and in the early 1870s was a professional in Bradford. While there he played against the United South and made the right impact by bowling W.G. Grace, a feat which made the county authorities take note. In 1873 he played his first game for the white rose and thus began an association with first-class cricket that spanned two decades.

A tall, beefy opening batter, Ulyett was 'a powerful smiter' of a cricket ball, as Lord Hawke once described his approach. His style at times was unorthodox, even freakish, and some of his mightiest shots have lived on down the generations, such as the blow at Lord's in 1878 that carried 109 yards. His strokes were played with the backing of enormous power, particularly his drives, and met with the warm appreciation of those who followed the Victorian Tyke. His opening partnerships with the dour Louis Hall were a feature of Yorkshire cricket at the time.

Individually Ulyett made 15 hundreds for the county and he carried his bat during his career-best 199 not out at Bramall Lane in 1887. His three best seasons with the willow for Yorkshire were 1878, when he made 1,083 runs, 1882 when he reached 1,158 and 1887 with 1,285. In first-class cricket he passed the 1,000 run landmark in ten seasons and in 1883 made 1,562 runs at an average of 31.87. Up until the time of his death he was considered the best batsman the county had ever produced.

Primarily thought of as a batsman, Ulyett was also a fast bowler who could move the ball back in sharply. He chose to bowl quickly throughout his long career, never really changing the basic concept of fast-medium deliveries. Just over 450 wickets for Yorkshire were obtained at an economical average and his best match figures (12 for 102) were taken against Lancashire at Huddersfield in 1889. In the field he was excellent anywhere and he once took a

The Yorkshire team of 1884, for whom George Ulyett was a major performer. From left to right, back row: E. Peate, T. Emmett, H. Turner (scorer), W. Harris, J. Hunter. Middle row: J.T. Rawlin, F. Lee, L. Hall (captain), R. Peel, G. Ulyett. Front row: W. Bates, I. Grimshaw.

catch off the giant Australian batsman George Bonnor that many considered he was foolish to even attempt.

Ulyett played in the inaugural 'Test Match' in 1877 and also had the unique distinction of appearing in South Africa's first Test match during the 1888/89 tour of the country. In all he toured Australia five times. At Sydney during the 1881/82 tour he and R.G.Barlow shared the first century opening partnership in Test cricket. In the Melbourne Test during that same series, Ulyett's 149 (his only Test century) was the first Test hundred for England in Australia. His all-round status was also confirmed at the highest level; his 50 Test scalps cost 20.40 apiece and his seven for 36 at Lord's in 1884 helped see off the Australians by an innings and five runs.

Ulyett's jocular nature made him a 'prince of practical jokers'. He is reputed to have filled the socks of Yorkshire colleague Tom Emmett with snails. On another occasion, pretending to be deaf, he, with Ted Peate as his minder, somehow got into a reception given by Prime Minister Gladstone at 10 Downing Street. He enjoyed his moments of fun both on and off the field and when asked what he thought of the next generation of cricketers that followed his playing days he commented: 'Present day cricketers walk up to the wickets looking as serious as if they were going to church. When they have made a duck they walk back as if they had been touched in a tender spot by the parson.'

Despite his benefit match in 1887 being completed in two days, the popular Ulyett finally received a round three figure sum to sustain him in later life. He did some umpiring in retirement and was landlord of the Vine Hotel in Pitsmoor before his untimely death in June 1898. Having caught a chill whilst attending the county game at Bramall Lane, he never recovered. Despite very heavy rain an estimated 4,000 people attended his funeral at Burngreave cemetery.

Somehow Ulyett found time during his sporting career to play in goal for Sheffield Wednesday, no doubt in the same cheerful manner that epitomised his cricket. This warm, honest joker never belied the nickname given to him by his Yorkshire colleagues; he remained 'Happy Jack' to the end.

Michael Vaughan

RHB and OB, 1993-present

Full Name: Michael Paul Vaughan
Birth: Salford, 29/10/1974

Type of Player: Opening right-hand batsman, right-arm off-break bowler

First Class Career for Yorkshire:
Debut: v. Lancashire, Old Trafford, 1993
Matches: 117
Batting: 7,327 runs (Av. 36.45), 17 centuries. Highest Score: 183 v. Glamorgan, Sophia Gardens, Cardiff, 1996
Bowling: 85 wkts (Av. 47.07). Best performance: 4-39 v. Oxford University, The Parks, 1994
Fielding: 45 catches

Tests: 9, 1999-2000/01

One of the most elegant of Yorkshire's opening batsmen, Michael Vaughan was the first English player to benefit from the county's decision to abandon the unwritten Yorkshire-born only policy. Vaughan moved to Sheffield with his parents at the age of nine, attended Silverdale School, played for Sheffield Collegiate and gained a place at the Academy. He captained England at both Under-17 and Under-19 level, the latter in Sri Lanka and at home against India, when he averaged 50.16 in the three 'Tests'.

On entry into Yorkshire's first team, Vaughan was immediately given an opening berth, with Moxon, and responded with a half-century on debut, against Lancashire. Their first century stand came in the first game of 1994 – also against Lancashire – and Vaughan's own first century soon followed, at The Parks. With two further centuries the season ended with him having passed the 1,000-run mark.

There followed a few years during which Vaughan consolidated his position in the county side with some very consistent performances, his best season being 1995 with 1,244 runs at 32.73. However, his further international prospects began to look bleak as he endured two very poor tours with England 'A'. The turning point came with his third such tour and election as captain for the trip to South Africa and Zimbabwe in 1998/99. Not only was the team victorious in its two series, but Vaughan created a most favourable impression with his man-management skills as well as his mature and adaptable batting.

Vaughan's Test debut one year later was a true baptism of fire as he took guard at Johannesburg with the score standing at 2 for 4. His response was to accumulate a fighting innings and impress with his composure and cool temperament, something that he has shown throughout his Test career thus far. He has played three match-winning innings and won two match awards, his highest score being 76 at Headingley against the West Indies. Vaughan is a player who has allied steel to his stylish stroke-play and he gives the appearance of having plenty of time in which to play the ball – the true sign of a quality player.

Before the increase in international cricket Vaughan was widely seen as Byas's successor to the Yorkshire captaincy. He has now been given the burdensome FEC label in some quarters; as he gradually establishes himself in the Test side this may not be an impossible target for this courteous and modest cricketer.

Hedley Verity

RHB and SLA, 1930-1939

Full Name: Hedley Verity
Birth: Headingley, Leeds, 18/05/1905
Death: Caserta, Italy, 31/07/1943

Type of Player: Lower order right-hand batsman, left-arm slow medium bowler

First Class Career for Yorkshire:
Debut: v. Sussex, Fartown, Huddersfield, 1930
Matches: 278
Batting: 3,898 runs (Av. 17.96), 1 century.
Highest Score: 101 v. Jamaica, Sabina Park, 1935/36
Bowling: 1,558 wkts (Av. 13.70), 5wi 141 times.
Best performance: 10-10 v. Nottinghamshire, Headingley, 1932
Fielding: 191 catches
Year of last match: 1939

Tests: 40, 1931-1939

A craftsman amongst slow left-arm bowlers of the 1930s, Hedley Verity forged, in a relatively brief career, the next golden link in Yorkshire's rich chain of spinners. As the successor to his own mentor, Wilfred Rhodes, Verity inherited a heavy burden of expectation, but in every respect it was one he was equal to.

Born not far from Headingley cricket ground, Verity was raised in Rawdon where his father was a coal merchant and lay preacher. A conscientious pupil, he played cricket at Yeadon and Guisley Secondary School and when only fourteen scored 47 and took seven wickets in a match for Rawdon first team.

His route to the Yorkshire dressing room took him from his local club via Horsforth Hall Park and onwards to the Lancashire League in order to further his apprenticeship. Warwickshire did not take up Verity's services after a trial at Edgbaston in 1928 and he had reached the age of twenty-five when he played his maiden county game for Yorkshire. Rhodes, at the age of fifty-two, had just announced his intention to retire. Sixty-four wickets in that first season at a cost of 12.42 runs apiece made Verity nothing more than a promising newcomer. The real deluge of wickets began in earnest in 1931.

In all matches for Yorkshire he captured 169 wickets and 188 in all first-class cricket, at an average of 13.52. At the top of the county bowling averages, only Larwood was above him in the national figures. Verity became the second Yorkshire bowler, 17 years after Alonzo Drake had first performed the deed, to take all ten wickets in an innings when, on his twenty-sixth birthday, he claimed 10 for 36 against Warwickshire at Headingley. He made his Test debut that year at The Oval against New Zealand and was selected, along with his county colleague Bill Bowes as one of *Wisden*'s five Cricketers of the Year.

In July 1932 Verity performed a feat that in bowling terms placed him among the 'immortals'. His figures of 10 for 10 in Nottinghamshire's second innings remains the best analysis for all first-class cricket. The ten poor Nottinghamshire batsmen were dismissed in the space of 52 balls and he ended matters with seven wickets in 15 deliveries, including a hat-trick.

Verity used his height to extract additional bounce from the pitch and his control of spin and flight, allied to subtle variations in pace and length, left even the best batsmen unsettled by his skills. On wet or sticky wickets he would reduce his pace and throw

A young Hedley Verity, pictured before his debut for Yorkshire CCC.

his leg-spinner even higher. Yet even when bowling at his slowest there was diversity in his speed and a brisk yorker or fast inswinger could be called upon to surprise a hapless opponent. He went about his work with a calm and quiet composure, as his county captain Brian Sellers related: 'His character and disposition never changed amid all his triumphs; he just remained Hedley Verity. He was an ideal fellow and a charming personality. His bowling action indicated his character; no fuss, hurry or rush. He worked hard all day with steadiness and determination.' A style that was to bring him 1,956 first-class wickets at less than 15 apiece.

On seven occasions he took nine wickets in an innings – all for Yorkshire – to go with his two 'all ten' returns. Notable among those was nine for 12 against Kent at Dover in 1936. In all first-class cricket, 164 times he took five or more wickets in an innings and captured ten or more in a match, 54 times. He passed 100 wickets in nine seasons, going on to 200 or more in 1935, 1936 and 1937. The statistics remain awe-inspiring. When not bowling out sides for Yorkshire and England, Verity contributed both in the field, where he was a good close-in-fielder, and with the bat.

R.C. Robertson-Glasgow, when describing Verity's batting, wrote: 'A casual observer might have mistaken Verity for Sutcliffe a little out of form...' Relied upon to hold up one end, he played correctly. In 1936 he came close to performing the double, making 855 runs at an average of nearly 32 and did in fact open the batting for England on the 1936/37 tour of Australia.

The real examination of Verity's quality came at Test level where his battles with Don Bradman became fabled. Fourteen Australian wickets in a day at Lord's in 1934 remained the pinnacle of his deeds for England. Bradman's own tribute to Verity suggested that Australia's greatest batsman never fully mastered the Yorkshire left-armer: 'Although opposed to him in many Tests, I could never claim to have completely fathomed his strategy, for it was never static nor mechanical.' Verity dismissed Bradman eight times in Tests – more than any other bowler and ten times in first-class cricket – a record equal to Clarrie Grimmett's. Verity's final Test record rested at 144 wickets (average 24.37).

Mortally wounded leading his Green Howards company into battle in Sicily and moved to an Italian hospital, Verity died in Caserta on the last day of July 1943. He was buried with full military honours. In September 1944 a cricket match took place at Roundhay Park in Leeds and those who had played with and against him gathered to honour the memory of a cricketer who achieved so much in only a fleeting decade at the top.

Abram Waddington

RHB and LFM, 1919-1927

Full Name: Abraham Waddington (known as Abram)
Birth: Clayton, Bradford, 04/02/1893
Death: Throxenby, Scarborough, 28/10/1959

Type of Player: Tail end right-hand batsman, left-arm fast medium bowler

First Class Career for Yorkshire:
Debut: v. Derbyshire, Chesterfield, 1919
Matches: 255
Batting: 2,396 runs (Av. 12.95), 1 century.
Highest Score: 114 v. Worcestershire, Headingley, 1927
Bowling: 835 wkts (Av. 19.40), 5wi 51 times.
Best performance: 8-34 v. Northamptonshire, Headingley, 1922
Fielding: 222 catches
Year of last match: 1927
Tests: 2, 1920/21

A highly competitive character, 'Abe' Waddington was a cricketer with attitude. His bowling made an immediate and dramatic first impression for the county in their Championship winning season of 1919. He made his debut at Chesterfield in early July, took 4 for 26 in Derbyshire's 87 all out, and ended his first season with 100 wickets at 18.74 apiece. Crossley Hall and Sandy Lane in the West Bradford League were Waddington's early clubs, although his reputation gathered momentum before World War One, with Lidget Green and then Laisterdyke, champions of the Bradford League in 1913.

The war thwarted his chances of representing Yorkshire before 1914 and he was twenty-six years of age when county cricket got underway again. Waddington's second season in 1920 brought an even better tally of wickets – 141 (average 16.79) with two impressive match performances at Hull (12 for 74) against Leicestershire and at Northampton (13 for 48). In the later match against Northamptonshire, he and Emmott Robinson bowled unchanged throughout. In one spell the left-armer took four wickets in five balls including a hat-trick. That same summer he also took seven wickets in an innings against Warwickshire (7 for 21).

He hurried batsman with his speed, particularly in his early days. A fluent, rhythmical bowler with a curving approach to the wicket, he kept a good length and was capable of swerve and awkward bounce from the pitch. Beneath the elegance though was a volatile temperament and fickle attitude that got him into trouble on more than one occasion. Selected to tour Australia under J.W.H.T. Douglas in 1920/21, he played in two Tests but without any success; his solitary wicket cost him 119 runs. England lost a catastrophic series 5-0 and Waddington's Test career was already at an end. He fought back for Yorkshire in 1921 and 1922 passing 100 wickets in both seasons.

Injuries were a cruel feature of Waddington's time with Yorkshire. At Huddersfield in 1923 on a wet outfield he fell and injured ligaments in his arm and missed the rest of the season. Later a troublesome shoulder injury hastened retirement. He played his final match in 1927 and his 852 first-class wickets cost him 19.75 each. A year later he received a grant of £1,000 from the Club. A reliable fielder and useful batsman, he did score one first-class century, in his last season. In other sporting arenas, Waddington played in goal for Bradford City and Halifax Town at football and was a skilful golfer. No doubt he played both games with the same passion and fire that typified his cricket.

Ted Wainwright

RHB and RM/OB, 1888-1902

Full Name: Edward Wainwright*
Birth: Tinsley, Sheffield, 08/04/1865
Death: Sheffield, 28/10/1919

Type of Player: Middle order right-hand batsman, right-arm medium pace/off-break bowler

First Class Career for Yorkshire:
Debut: v. MCC, Lord's, 1888
Matches: 355
Batting: 11,130 runs (Av. 21.44), 18 centuries.
Highest Score: 228 v. Surrey, The Oval, 1899
Bowling: 1,007 wkts (Av. 17.12), 5wi 59 times.
Best performance: 9-66 v. Middlesex, Bramall Lane, Sheffield, 1894
Fielding: 334 catches
Year of last match: 1902

Tests: 5, 1893-1897/98

A tall, craggy player from Sheffield, Edward (Ted) Wainwright, with his rich Yorkshire humour, was an important all-round professional in Lord Hawke's six Championship winning sides between 1893 and 1902. Elder brother of Walker Wainwright, who played 24 times for Yorkshire between 1903 and 1905, Ted began his cricket with local club, Tinsley – a long way from his county debut at Lord's in 1888.

An off-break bowler, he turned the ball appreciably and on a sticky or helpful track his spin was described by A.W. Pullin as 'prodigious'. On dryer pitches he was less effective and *Wisden* made one other criticism of his technique: 'Had his command of length been as strong as his spin and break he might have ranked as one of the greatest of bowlers.' A sound batsman whose best strokes were the cut and off-drive, he was an accomplished slip fielder alongside the brilliant John Tunnicliffe.

As a Test cricketer, Wainwright's record was ordinary. His five Test caps brought only 132 runs (average 14.66) and not even one wicket. The good, hard Australian surfaces did not suit him and, unable to turn the ball there, he went immediately to Bramall Lane on his return and, without removing his coat, bowled a delivery that 'broke a foot', much to the delight of a relieved Wainwright. The intense Australian heat on the 1897/98 tour added to his woes.

Wainwright's lasting reputation was established with Yorkshire. He launched his career in his maiden season, hitting 105 against the 1888 Australians at Bradford, in June. He passed 1,000 runs in a season three times, in 1897,1899 and 1901. At the Oval in August 1899, he and George Hirst added 340 for the fifth wicket in three and a half hours batting together. The quality of the wicket was underlined when Wainwright's career best 228 was surpassed by Surrey's Tom Hayward with 273.

His all-round form in 1897 secured him the double, with 1,612 runs and 101 wickets; a benefit season, raising £1,800, was enjoyed a year later. His best season with the ball was 1894 (166 wickets, average 12.73). At Dewsbury he captured 13 for 38 against Sussex which included taking the last five wickets in seven balls; a hat-trick formed part of that final destructive spell. He did take all ten wickets in one innings for Yorkshire but the game, against Staffordshire in 1890, was not considered first-class and nine Middlesex wickets at Bramall Lane, again in 1894, was his 'official' career best.

Neville Cardus immortalised Ted Wainwright as Shrewsbury School's coach in his book *Close of Play*, recalling his days as assistant professional to one of the county's most engaging characters.

Johnny Wardle

LHB and SLA, 1946-1958

Full Name: John Henry Wardle
Birth: Ardsley, Barnsley, 08/01/1923
Death: Hatfield, Doncaster, 23/07/1985

Type of Player: Lower order left-hand batsman, slow left-arm orthodox/googly bowler

First Class Career for Yorkshire:
Debut: v. Worcestershire, Headingley, 1946
Matches: 330
Batting: 5,765 runs (Av. 15.96). Highest Score: 79 v.Lancashire, Old Trafford, 1951
Bowling: 1,539 wkts (Av. 18.13), 5wi 117 times. Best performance: 9-25 v. Lancashire, Old Trafford, 1954
Fielding: 210 catches
Year of last match: 1958

Tests: 28, 1947/48-1957

A bowling genius of both conformist and unorthodox methods, Johnny Wardle wore his White Rose with great pride. A single-minded pursuit of excellence drove his bowling to high level, whilst his comic antics and wit on the field reflected the other side of his approach to life and cricket. From the age of four, Wardle grew up in the village of Brampton between Rotherham and Barnsley. He played cricket at the local junior school and Wath-on-Dearne Grammar School, having won a scholarship to the latter. Such was the youngster's appetite for the game, and living so close to the colliery cricket ground, he was soon turning out for Brampton in the South Yorkshire or Mexborough Evening Leagues.

After leaving grammar school he took a position as an apprentice fitter at Hickleton Main Colliery, which allowed him time to devote to cricket. His sporting skills though were varied; a good rugby full-back at school, he was a quick and clever left-winger at soccer. He did have trials with Wolverhampton Wanderers but instead established a name and a presence in local cricket that, despite the war, drew the county's attention. As a seventeen-year-old in 1940, he bowled Rockingham out by himself ending with figures of ten for 36. Before the war ended he produced a record crop of 113 wickets at 7.85 runs each for Denaby in the Yorkshire Council.

The loss of Hedley Verity in 1943 left an immediate vacancy for a left-arm slow bowler in the county ranks when cricket got underway once again in 1945. The veteran Arthur Booth, who had played his first match for Yorkshire in 1931, initially claimed the place and in 1946 took 111 wickets at 11.61 each. Wardle made his debut that season and in 1947 edged out Alan Mason to claim the left-armer's spot for himself. By August he had won his county cap, and his 86 first-class wickets that summer cost him 25.46 each. Called upon to get through a lot of work for Yorkshire following the retirement of Booth, Bowes and Smailes – he bowled in excess of 1,300 overs in 1948 – he took 150 first-class wickets that year and 100 or more in each of the following nine English seasons. His best returns for Yorkshire were in 1950, when his 172 wickets were taken at an average of 16.30, and in 1955 when he took 195 first-class wickets at 16.14 each.

A more than useful late order batsman who was prepared to hit the ball hard and high, Wardle was also a good, keen close

Johnny Wardle pictured in his MCC blazer at the Scarborough Cricket Festival in 1955.

fielder. A man of spontaneous humour, he seemed to have a natural understanding of the crowd's mood, especially at Bramall Lane where he played the showman more than anywhere. A conjurer with the cricket ball, Wardle bowled the traditional left-arm ball as decreed in Yorkshire and sometimes, with a high degree of control, the wrist spinner's googly and chinaman less accepted in the shires.

The England selectors' preference for Surrey's Tony Lock confined Wardle to only 28 appearances for his country, something which rankled with him throughout a period when Lock's faster ball was considered illegal by many except, it seemed, the authorities. Wardle toured the West Indies under 'Gubby' Allen in 1947/48 but, with very little experience to call on, didn't make any significant contribution and bowled only three overs in his Test debut at Trinidad. He played in three of the Tests against Australia in 1953 and in the closing stages of the Old Trafford Test took 4 for 7 when Australia collapsed to 35 for 8. His reward was to be replaced for the last two Tests by, of course, Lock.

Another touch of irony in the Lock/Wardle debate occurred in 1954 when the Yorkshireman was selected alongside his great rival amongst *Wisden*'s five Cricketers of the Year. The tour of South Africa in the winter of 1956/57 brought Wardle the greatest acclaim in international cricket. Bowling mainly out of the back of the hand, he took 26 wickets in four Tests at 13.80 each, including 12 for 89 in the Second Test at Cape Town and 90 wickets on the tour at 12.25 apiece. Few would have thought that after his match winning bowling in South Africa, Wardle would play only once more for England – at Lord's against West Indies in 1957. His 102 Test wickets were taken at an average of 20.39.

Throughout the 1950s there were many talented individuals in the Yorkshire dressing room and several hard temperaments that lacked a binding influence. That changed in 1958 with the arrival of new captain Ronnie Burnet. The decision by Yorkshire to release Wardle, shortly after an invitation to tour Australia with the MCC had arrived, sparked an immediate reproach by the crestfallen senior pro. His scathing comments in the *Daily Mail* brought a swift and tragic conclusion to Wardle's career. The wounds were healed much later.

He became an Honorary Life Member of Yorkshire in 1970, helped Geoff Cope to restructure his bowling action a little later and shortly before his premature death in 1985 was appointed as the Club's bowling consultant. A total professional, Wardle knew more about the art of bowling than most; his 1,846 first-class wickets remain as testimony to his brilliance.

Willie Watson

LHB and RM, 1939-1957

Full Name: Willie Watson
Birth: Bolton-on-Dearne, Rotherham, 07/03/1920

Type of Player: Middle order left-hand batsman, right-arm medium pace bowler

First Class Career for Yorkshire:
Debut: v. Nottinghamshire, Bramall Lane, Sheffield, 1939
Matches: 283
Batting: 13,953 runs (Av. 38.22), 26 centuries.
Highest Score: 214* v. Worcestershire, Worcester, 1955
Bowling: 0 wkts
Fielding: 170 catches
Year of last match: 1957

Tests: 23, 1951-1958/59

The name of Willie Watson will forever be associated with the dramatic rearguard action which he fought with Trevor Bailey at Lord's in 1953 against Australia. It was Watson's first Ashes Test and, in scoring 109 in almost six hours, he completed his first Test century in his seventh such game. Their stand of 163 lasted for over four hours on the final day and ensured that Australia could not force the victory that was expected when Watson had come to the wicket with the score on 12 for 3. His highest Test score, 116 against the West Indies at Kingston in the following winter, was his only other Test century. He never really established himself in the side, however, and eventually concluded his England career with 879 runs at an average of only 25.85. Cricket at Royds Hall Grammar School and for Paddock was followed by three successive ducks on his debut for the county second XI, but he established himself in the full Yorkshire side after 1945 as the left-hander to succeed Leyland.

Watson played in a fluent, handsome style and had a calm temperament. He had all the strokes at his command and could adapt his game to the situation, even to the extent of appearing in all of the top six batting positions in his Test career. Watson was fortunate in being able to combine careers in two sports. He was a double-international, gaining four soccer caps for England, and the 1950 cricket season was the only one in which he did not score 1,000 runs, this being because of his involvement in the World Cup.

He left Yorkshire after the 1957 season, having received £5,356 from his 1956 benefit, and embarked on several successful seasons with Leicestershire, captaining them in four campaigns from 1958. His best season was 1959, when he accumulated 2,212 runs at 55.30. His highest score of 257 was for MCC against British Guiana on the 1953/54 tour being the best of his three double-centuries.

His career ended with 25,670 runs at 39.86, including 55 centuries. In 1962 he became a Test selector but six years later emigrated to become a coach in Johannesburg. 30 June 1953 was Watson's greatest hour as the country followed his progress intently. It ensured his selection as one of the *Wisden* five for 1954, but more importantly, as one of the heroes in an Ashes-winning series.

Craig White

RHB and RFM, 1990-present

Full Name: Craig White
Birth: Morley, 16/12/1969

Type of Player: Middle order right-hand batsman, right-arm fast medium bowler

First Class Career for Yorkshire:
Debut: v. Northamptonshire, Headingley, 1990
Matches: 142
Batting: 5,928 runs (Av. 31.53), 8 centuries. Highest Score: 181 v.Lancashire, Headingley, 1996
Bowling: 234 wkts (Av. 26.83), 5wi 6 times. Best performance: 8-55 v. Gloucestershire, King's School Ground, Gloucester, 1998
Fielding: 103 catches

Tests: 18, 1994-2000/01

Although born in Yorkshire, Craig White was raised and educated in Australia before a return to his native county in 1990 on a cricket scholarship kick-started his first-class career. There were understandable grounds for 'Chalky' White to be considered a fully fledged 'Aussie', as he played for their national Under-17 and Under-19 sides. Still, his West Yorkshire origins were undisputable and he made his First XI debut before he had even appeared in the second team, as Trueman did. He did little on debut but topped the county Second XI batting averages in 1990 with 469 runs in three matches, including 209 and 115 not out in the Worcester match.

Back in Victoria, White had been firstly a wicketkeeper, which has served Yorkshire at times as a stand-in for Blakey, then a right-handed batsman who bowled off-spinners. The bowling style changed from spin to fast-medium around 1993. Generating speed from a relaxed run-up and quick arm action, White hits the deck hard and at times hurries the best batsmen.

Chairman of selectors Raymond Illingworth must be credited for spotting White's potential. He was the surprise selection for the First Test at Trent Bridge in 1994, having won his county cap the previous season. An innings of 51 at Lord's and 3 for 18 at Old Trafford, both against New Zealand, suggested further consideration. Selected for England's 1994/95 tour of Australia, he did not feature in the Test rubber.

In addition to batting in the top six for Yorkshire and being first change bowler in Championship cricket, White is an important part of the county's one-day side, and most of his international involvement has been in that format. In the one-day series against South Africa and Zimbabwe in 1999/2000, replacing injured Andrew Flintoff, he won the Man of the Match award at Bulawayo, taking 5 for 21 and scoring an important 26 against Zimbabwe.

Many pundits were surprised to see White's name amongst the 12 England players awarded a central contract at the start of the 2000 season, but the all-rounder repayed the faith shown in him by Nasser Hussain and Duncan Fletcher, helping England's victory in the triangular one-day series and the Tests against the West Indies.

His lively pace, particularly bowling around the wicket at the West Indian left-handed batsmen, brought him his first five wicket haul in Test cricket, on his home ground in the Fourth Test, in England's sensational two-day win. He improved his Test best figures to 5 for 32 in the final match of the series at The Oval. Major contributions on England's tours to Pakistan and Sri Lanka in 2000/01 suggest that White will be in the national side for some time to come.

Benjamin Wilson

RHB and RFM, 1906-1914

Full Name: Benjamin Birdsall Wilson
Birth: Scarborough, 11/12/1879
Death: Harrogate, 14/09/1957

Type of Player: Opening right-hand batsman, right-arm fast medium bowler

First Class Career for Yorkshire:
Debut: v. Kent, Catford, 1906
Matches: 185
Batting: 8,053 runs (Av. 27.21), 15 centuries. Highest Score: 208 v. Sussex, Park Avenue, Bradford, 1914
Bowling: 2 wkts (Av. 139.00). Best performance: 1-16 v. Somerset, Bath, 1909
Fielding: 53 catches
Year of last match: 1914

Tests: Nil

A resolute and determined batsman, Benjamin Wilson never made the most of the talent at his disposal. Too often undue caution was a feature of his play when, with height and build, he was capable of batting in a far more fluent style. Had he thrown off the shackles that impeded him, Wilson might have gone on to prove himself in the top rank of Yorkshire opening batsmen. Wilson joined Scarborough cricket club at the age of seventeen as an aspiring bowler. His batting, though, showed the greatest promise; he became a reliable, if dour, opening batsman for them and in the year of his county debut, 1906, he averaged 44.6 for Scarborough.

Wilson was twenty-six when he first appeared in the Yorkshire First XI and it took the stocky right-hander two years before he made his first century (109 against Derbyshire in 1908). However, a year later he added a further three centuries to his tally in the space of three weeks and passed 1,000 runs in a season for the first time. His most consistent seasons were between 1911 and 1914. In each of those years he scored in excess of 1,400 runs, his best in 1914 (1,608 runs at an average of 32.74) and made his last four hundreds for the county. His double century (208) against Sussex at Bradford that summer was also his career highest.

Occasionally Wilson emerged from his guarded mode, as in 1912 when he and Schofield Haigh put on a 'brilliant forcing display', scoring 108 to beat Lancashire who had set Yorkshire 217 to win in 145 minutes. But too often his negative approach attracted criticism. In 1912 *Wisden* wrote: 'Here is a batsman who presents a puzzle to the critics. No one without great natural powers could have made the big scores he has obtained for Yorkshire during the past few seasons, and yet he has not gained for himself an assured position. Possessing every physical advantage, he is at his best a very fine hitter, but he is apt, for no reason whatever, to subside into laborious slowness, and he is too fond of stopping the ball with his legs.'

The re-start of cricket, after World War One, in 1919 came too late for Wilson. In his fortieth year and facing derogatory comments about his batting, he was released by Yorkshire with a grant of £250. He coached for over a decade at Harrow and later went to St Peter's School in York. His son, Ben, had trials with Yorkshire and played for Warwickshire in 1951. Only Wilson's 'self-imposed limitations' and the onset of the Great War prevented him from becoming John Tunnicliffe's long term successor at the top of Yorkshire's batting line-up.

Don Wilson

LHB and SLA, 1957-1974

Full Name: Donald Wilson
Birth: Settle, 07/08/1937

Type of Player: Tail end left-hand batsman, slow left-arm bowler

First Class Career for Yorkshire:
Debut: v. Scotland, Whitehaugh, Paisley, 1957
Matches: 392
Batting: 5,788 runs (Av. 13.88). Highest Score: 83 v. Surrey, Bramall Lane, Sheffield, 1960
Bowling: 1,104 wkts (Av. 20.49), 5wi 46 times. Best performance: 7-19 v. MCC, Scarborough, 1969
Fielding: 235 catches
Year of last match: 1974

Tests: 6, 1963/64-1970/71

Nicknamed 'Mad Jack' in the Yorkshire dressing room, Don Wilson was a popular bowler from the Dales who took up Wardle's mantle. He played his cricket with a terrific enthusiasm and sense of fun. A tall (6 ft, 3 in.), lanky lad from Settle, he was captain of the school cricket side at Ingleton Secondary Modern. A carpenter's apprentice, he was recommended to Yorkshire by Len Hutton. Ted Lester, captain of the county Second XI, wrote at the end of the 1958 season: 'Throughout the season he [Wilson] has maintained an excellent length, flighted the ball intelligently and has attacked the whole time. His enthusiasm knows no bounds.' Those comments captured Wilson's outlook on cricket; he played it in an unmistakably buoyant manner and believed no goal was unachievable.

The season of 1968 was his best, when his 815.5 first-class overs brought him 109 wickets at just over 13 apiece and third spot in the national bowling averages. He took 100 wickets in a season five times and in 1966 became only the third Yorkshire bowler – after Macaulay in 1933 and Freeman in 1868 – to take two hat-tricks in the same season. Superb in the field, Wilson was also a dashing late-order batsman who played a memorable part in ensuring victory over Worcestershire in 1961. Chasing 190 to win, Yorkshire were 154 for 9 when Wilson, with his left-arm in plaster from elbow to knuckles because of a fractured thumb, joined Platt. Wilson, batting one-handed, finished 29 not out and an unlikely one-wicket win was secured.

The presence of Derek Underwood restricted Wilson to only six Test appearances although he did tour Australia, New Zealand, India and Sri Lanka. His 11 Test wickets, spread over almost eight years, cost him 42 runs each. His one first-class century, 112 against South Zone, was made whilst on the MCC tour of India in 1963/64. This popular slow-man received a benefit season in 1972, which raised £7,621.

His infectious love of the game took him into coaching following his retirement from first-class cricket, and after a spell in South Africa he became the head coach at Lord's from 1977 until 1990. After 13 years in London he returned to North Yorkshire to take up a position as Director of Sport at Ampleforth College. Few players or coaches can have put as much back into cricket as the happy practitioner Don Wilson.

Rockley Wilson

RHB and SRA, 1899-1923

Full Name: Evelyn Rockley Wilson
Birth: Balsterstone, Sheffield, 25/03/1879
Death: Winchester, Hampshire, 21/07/1957

Type of Player: Middle/lower order right-hand batsman, right-arm slow bowler

First Class Career for Yorkshire:
Debut: v. Somerset, Anlaby Road, Hull, 1899
Matches: 66
Batting: 902 runs (Av. 16.70), 1 century. Highest Score: 104* v. Essex, Park Avenue, Bradford, 1913
Bowling: 197 wkts (Av. 15.76), 5wi 12 times. Best performance: 7-32 v. Middlesex, Bramall Lane, Sheffield, 1921
Fielding: 30 catches
Year of last match: 1923

Tests: 1, 1920/21

One of the most extraordinary, as well as lengthy, careers of any cricketer belonged to the colourful Rockley Wilson. He played for Yorkshire in two distinct spells, answered a crisis after the First World War and won his only Test cap at the age of forty-one! Wilson undertook coaching from Emmett while at Rugby, where he was captain in 1897, and went up to Cambridge in 1899. His first-class debut was for A.J. Webbe's XI against the university, scoring 117 not out and 70, and he gained a blue for all four of his years there, again being captain in his final season. He led Cambridge to victory over Oxford by five wickets, his contribution including eight wickets. In the previous year he had scored 118 and taken five for 71. He opened the batting or the bowling in all four of his Varsity matches.

As with all successful batsmen, Wilson had a sound technique but, in the spirit of an amateur in the 'Golden Age', he liked to attack the bowling, especially enjoying the hook stroke. His spin bowling was based on a low action, but he could move the ball both ways and possessed immaculate length and flight.

Wilson played in only nine games for Yorkshire until 1902 and a teaching appointment at Winchester prevented him playing again until 1913, when he appeared during the holidays. The loss of Booth and Drake made these appearances all the more vital after 1918 and he enjoyed the most successful period of his county career. Second place in the national bowling averages in 1920 (51 wickets at 19.11) secured a trip to Australia as vice-captain. What ensued, however, was considerable disappointment. He played in only the final Test and his aggregates for the first-class games were 124 runs and eight wickets. Pieces he wrote for the *Daily Express* led to a ban on cricketers writing for the press when on tour.

Wilson ended his first-class career with 3,565 runs (average 22.00) and 467 wickets (average 17.63). His highest score was 142 for Cambridge against MCC at Lord's in 1902 and his best bowling 7 for 16 for R.A. Bennett's Team against All West Indies at Georgetown in 1902. He was in charge of cricket at Winchester from 1904 until 1928, but his devotion to the game extended beyond his excellent coaching. He accumulated a large cricket library and became an authority on the history of the game.

Vic Wilson

LHB and RM, 1946-1962

Full Name: John Victor Wilson
Birth: Scampston, Malton, 17/01/1921

Type of Player: Middle order left-hand batsman, right-arm medium pace bowler

First Class Career for Yorkshire:
Debut: v. Warwickshire, Edgbaston, 1946
Matches: 477
Batting: 20,548 runs (Av. 31.66), 29 centuries. Highest Score: 230 v. Derbyshire, Bramall Lane, Sheffield, 1952
Bowling: 3 wkts (Av. 104.33). Best performance: 1-3 v. Derbyshire, Harrogate, 1951
Fielding: 520 catches
Year of last match: 1962

Tests: Nil

A momentous departure from tradition occurred in 1960 when Vic Wilson was appointed Yorkshire's captain. He was the first professional leader since 1883 but in terms of results, with two titles and a second place in his three seasons, he remains the county's most successful skipper. Wilson attended Norton Boys' and Malton Grammar schools. His first club was Malton but he also played for five others in the Yorkshire and Bradford leagues. He made one appearance for the county Second XI before the start of the Second World War but his chances improved later and 1948 brought his first century, against Surrey at The Oval, his first 1,000-run season and his county cap.

The hallmark of Wilson's batting was his power; he was not a stylish player but his height and strength enabled him to play in a resolute manner. He established himself at number three in a very strong top six and acted for many years as the focus of the innings. Although he was occasionally leaden-footed against quality spin bowling, he had a solid temperament and displayed consistency throughout most of his career. 1951 brought his best season as he scored 2,027 runs at 48.26 as well as taking 55 catches. He would surpass this with 61 in 1955 and it was his outstanding fielding, specialising at short-leg, which gained him a place on the tour to Australia in 1954/55. He was twelfth man for all five Tests and that was as near as he came to playing for England.

Wilson earned a well-deserved benefit of £5,758 in 1958 but this was also the year of Wardle's sacking and, as senior professional, he was needed to keep the team united behind the new skipper, Burnet. Despite loss of form in this and the following season, his status made him the natural choice for leader as the county entered a new and and highly successful era. His reward for winning the Championship in 1960 was selection as one of the *Wisden* five and although he tended to be unimaginative on the field of play, his resolution and the strength of the team brought regular victories.

Not one to avoid confrontation if necessary – he once sent Trueman home from Taunton for lateness – he retired at the age of forty-one, content in the knowledge that he had inherited a generally happy side and been able to keep it that way.

Arthur Wood

RHB and WK, 1927-1946

Full Name: Arthur Wood
Birth: Fagley, Bradford, 25/08/1898
Death: Middleton, Ilkley, 01/04/1973

Type of Player: Lower order right-hand batsman, wicketkeeper

First Class Career for Yorkshire:
Debut: v. Derbyshire, Chesterfield, 1927
Matches: 408
Batting: 8,579 runs (Av. 21.39), 1 century.
Highest Score: 123* v.Worcestershire, Bramall Lane, Sheffield, 1935
Bowling: 1 wkt (Av. 33.00). Best performance: 1-33 v. Jamaica, Sabina Park, 1935/36
Wicket-keeping: 612 catches, 243 stumpings
Year of last match: 1946

Tests: 4, 1938-1939

Every successful side has an outstanding wicketkeeper as its fulcrum and the 1930s Yorkshire team was highly fortunate in having the effervescent Arthur Wood. His ability to respond to the challenges set by as talented and varied trio of bowlers as Bowes, Verity and Macaulay meant that he is placed amongst the county's very best 'keepers. Wood proved himself while playing for Bradford and seized his chance for Yorkshire when Dolphin became an umpire. He was to play in 225 consecutive games, thus creating a Yorkshire record. A total of 1,249 runs at 30.46 in 1935 meant that he became the first Yorkshire 'keeper to score 1,000 runs in a season.

Unfortunate to be a contemporary of Les Ames and George Duckworth, Wood gained scant reward, in terms of Test caps, for his skill. He eventually made his England debut just five days before his fortieth birthday, went in to bat with the score on 770 for six and made 53 in a stand of 106 in 90 minutes. Caught and bowled from a full toss, he exclaimed, 'Trust me to lose my head in a crisis!'. Another remark which has often been repeated is, 'You've got him in two minds, he doesn't know whether to hit you for four or for six!'. Such encouragement was issued in Verity's direction when on the end of some hitting by Horace Cameron of South Africa.

Wood's humour was just part of a character which would rouse the team on its most difficult days. His 'keeping alone would have sufficed; however, its main feature was the cleanliness with which he took the ball. Despite his stocky build and squat figure, his agility, speed and dexterity defeated many an opponent. He was particularly brilliant down the leg side, and this was added to by the value of his batting, which should not be merely measured in quantity of runs but also in worth to the side. He could perform doggedly and determinedly but in a swashbuckling manner as well, whatever the needs of the team.

The adoring Yorkshire public responded with £2,563 for his 1939 benefit, the same year that he was one of the *Wisden* five. He was to play for just one more season after the war, helping the county to win his eighth Championship before the final break-up of a great side. It had been a team with Wood at its heart, doing a difficult job, day in, day out, with skill and humour.

Norman Yardley

RHB and RM, 1936-1955

Full Name: Norman Walter Dransfield Yardley
Birth: Gawber, Barnsley, 19/03/1915
Death: Lodge Moor, Sheffield, 04/10/1989

Type of Player: Middle order right-hand batsman, right-arm medium pace bowler

First Class Career for Yorkshire:
Debut: v. Derbyshire, Bramall Lane, Sheffield, 1936
Matches: 302
Batting: 11,632 runs (Av. 31.95), 17 centuries.
Highest Score: 183* v. Hampshire, Headingley, 1951.
Bowling: 195 wkts (Av. 29.83), 5wi twice.
Best performance: 6-106 v. MCC, Scarborough, 1952
Fielding: 220 catches
Year of last match: 1955

Tests: 20, 1938-1950

Norman Yardley took over the Yorkshire captaincy at a difficult time for the county. The rebuilding effort after the Second World War was not easy, and the last four years of his eight-year tenure, from 1948 to 1955, co-incided with the first four years of Surrey's total dominance of the County Championship. In addition, the Yorkshire squad contained some individuals with strong characters and these proved difficult to handle for a leader who, like his senior professional Hutton, was often involved with the England cause.

St.Peter's School, York was Yardley's main training ground in his youth. He topped the first XI batting averages three times and led the team in his fifth and final season, 1934, before going up to Cambridge. There he gained a blue for all four years and captained the University side in his final season (1938). He also gained a blue for hockey and, showing further evidence of all-round sporting prowess, was North of England squash champion on no less than six occasions.

Yardley played for the county second XI while still at school and soon developed into a hard-hitting batsman, good fielder and bowler of seamers that frustrated even the best batsmen. These included Bradman in particular, whose wicket was claimed three times by Yardley in consecutive Test innings in Australia in 1946/47. He first captained England at the end of this tour and did so in a total of 14 matches, his greatest success coming against the 1947 South Africans, with three wins and no defeat in the five Tests. This coincided with his best season as he scored 1,906 runs (average 44.32) and was rewarded with selection as one of the *Wisden* five. His Test career later concluded with totals of 812 runs (average 25.37) and 21 wickets (average 33.66).

He became a selector in 1951, acting as chairman for the first two of his three years, which concluded with the winning of the Ashes. Yardley's leadership of Yorkshire reflected the frustrations of those who were aware of the talents within the team but also its lack of collectivity and team spirit in aiming for the Championship title. He was perhaps too pleasant a person to deal with certain strong personalities but may have also been too orthodox and unimaginative on the field of play. He later became president of the Club, in the early 1980s, for three of the most difficult years in Yorkshire's history. He remained dignified and always acted as a true gentleman.